7⁹⁹

PROGRESSIVE
BASS GUITAR

GARY TURNER & BRENTON WHITE

60 MINUTE CASSETTE AVAILABLE

All the exercises in Progressive Bass Guitar have been recorded on to a 60 minute STEREO cassette tape.

Each exercise has been recorded in stereo to enable you to either listen to:

1. the Bass Guitar by itself (balance control fully to the left).
2. the Bass Guitar with backing band (balance control in mid-position.
3. the backing band only — to play along with (balance control fully to the right).

The drums are used to begin each exercise and to help you keep time.

THANK YOU –
JAMES STEWART (cover design)
STEPHANIE McCARRON (photographs)
PATRICK KELLY (music)
DAVID PARTINGTON (typesetting)
W.E.A., POLYGRAM, FESTIVAL, EMI, RCA, ASTOR (photographs)
and everyone else who helped along the way.

Distributed By

Australia

Koala Publications Pty. Ltd.
P.O. Box 140
Burnside 5066
South Australia
Ph (08) 268 1750
Fax 61-8-352 4760

U.S.A.

P.O. Box 27
3001 Redhill Ave.
Bldg. 2 # 221
Costa Mesa CA
U.S.A. 92626
Ph (714) 546 2743
Fax 1-714-546 2749

U.K. & EUROPE

Music Exchange
Unit 2,
Ringway Trading Estate,
Shadow Moss Road,
Wythenshawe,
Manchester M22 6LX,
Ph (061) 436 5110

ISBN 0 9595404 4 X

INDEX

INTRODUCTION

The bass guitarist, together with the drummer, form what is called the 'rhythm section' of a group. They create the backing beat, driving force and 'tightness' necessary for a successful group.

'Progressive Bass Guitar' will provide you with an essential guide to the riffs, scales, techniques and arpeggios used by bass guitarists. Within the three main sections of the book, a lesson by lesson structure has been used to give a clear and carefully graded method of study. No previous musical knowledge is assumed.

Aside from the specific aim of teaching bass guitar to enable you to play in a group, music theory is gradually introduced. This will help you to understand the material being presented and enable you to improvise and create your own bass lines.

From the beginning you should set yourself a goal. Many people learn bass guitar because of a desire to play like their favourite artist (e.g. Paul McCartney), or to play a certain style of music (e.g. rock, 'funk', reggae etc.). Motivations such as these will help you to persevere through the more difficult sections of work. As you develop it will be important to adjust and update your goals.

It is important to have a correct approach to practice. You will benefit more from several short practices (e.g. 15-30 minutes per day) than one or two long sessions per week. This is especially so in the early stages, because of the basic nature of the material being studied. In a practice session you should divide your time evenly between the study of new material and the revision of past work. It is a common mistake for semi-advanced students to practice only the pieces they can already play well. Although this is more enjoyable, it is not a very satisfactory method of practice. You should also endeavour to correct mistakes and experiment with new ideas.

You should combine the study of this book with constant experimentation and listening to other players. It is the authors' belief that the guidance of an experienced teacher will be an invaluable aid in your progress.

BEATLES (Courtesy EMI)

NOTATION

Two methods of music notation are presented in this book; namely notes and tablature. You need only use one of these methods*, whichever is most convenient (if you are not familiar with note reading follow the tablature outlined below).

TABLATURE

Tablature is a method of indicating the position of notes on the fretboard. There are four "tab" lines, each representing one of the four strings on the bass.

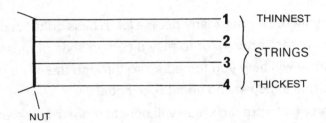

When a number is placed on one of the lines, it indicates the fret location of a note, e.g.

This indicates the 4th fret of the second string (an F# note).

This indicates the 7th fret of the 4th string (a B note).

This indicates the third string open (an A note).

The tablature, as used in this book, does not indicate the time values of the notes, only their position on the fretboard. You can read the time values by following the count written beneath the tablature, e.g.

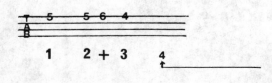

In this example the 1st note is worth 1 count, the 2nd and 3rd notes are worth ½ a count each and the 4th note is worth 2 counts.

The small number in the count is used to indicate where a note is being held or where a rest is being played.

* Note readers may need to refer to the tablature to determine the position of an exercise.

MUSIC NOTATION

The musical alphabet consists of 7 letters: **A B C D E F G**

Music is written on a staff, which consists of 5 parallel lines between which there are 4 spaces.

Music Staff

The Bass clef sign is placed at the beginning of each staff line.

Bass Clef.

This clef indicates the position of the note F which is on the line in between the two dots, (it is an old fashioned method of writing the letter F).

F note

The other lines and spaces on the staff are named as such:

Extra notes can be added by the use of short lines, called Ledger lines:

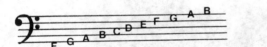

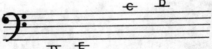

When a note is placed on the staff its head indicates its position, e.g.:

This is a B note

This is an E note.

When the note head is below the middle staff line the stem points upward and when the head is above the middle line the stem points downward. A note placed on the middle line (D) can have its stem pointing either up or down.

8

Bar lines are drawn across the staff, which divides the music into sections called Bars or Measures. A double bar line signifies either the end of the music, or the end of an important section of it.

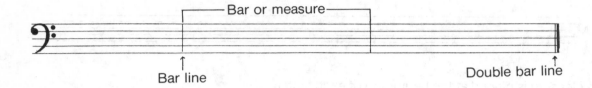

Bar or measure

Bar line   Double bar line

Two dots placed before a double bar line indicate that the music is to be repeated.

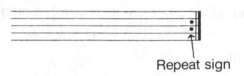

Repeat sign

ROLLING STONES (Courtesy EMI)

THE BASS GUITAR

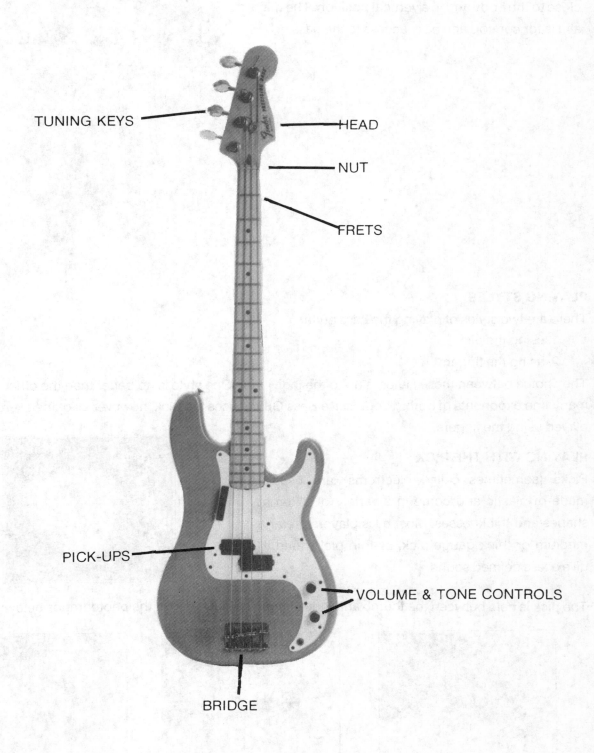

TUNING KEYS

HEAD

NUT

FRETS

PICK-UPS

VOLUME & TONE CONTROLS

BRIDGE

SEATING

Before you commence playing, a comfortable seating position is required. Most modern bass guitarists prefer to sit with their right leg raised, as shown in the photograph. The bass should be held close to the body and in a vertical position. The main aim is for comfort and easy access to the bass.

PLAYING STYLES

There are two styles of playing the bass guitar:

1. using the pick
2. using the fingers

The choice between these styles is up to the individual. One style is no better than the other as there are many fine exponents of both. 'Progressive Bass Guitar' uses the pick, however all of the exercises can be played using the fingers.

PLAYING WITH THE PICK

Picks (sometimes called plectrums) are usually made of plastic and come in a variety of different shapes and thicknesses. Most bass players prefer a medium or thick gauge pick, as thin picks tend to give a less defined sound.

The pick is held between the thumb and index finger, as illustrated in the photographs below:

1. Index finger curved.

2. Pick placed on index finger with its point about ¼ inch (1 cm) past the finger-tip.

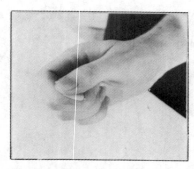

3. Thumb clamps down, holding the pick in place.

The correct position of the right hand is as such:

Playing with the pick creates a more crisp and treble sound than playing with the fingers.

PLAYING WITH THE FINGERS

When playing with the fingers, only the
index (i) and middle (m) fingers are used.

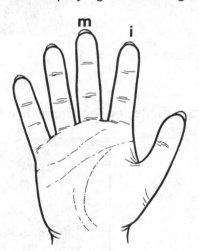

i = index

m = middle

When playing notes, the i and m fingers alternate and the rest stroke is used. The rest stroke involves the finger picking the string and then coming to rest on the next string. The diagram below illustrates the movement of the fingers in playing the rest stroke.

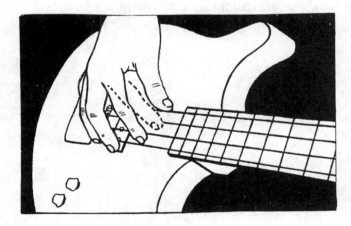

The thumb is not used for playing notes, but supports the hand by resting on or near the 4th string. The position of the right hand is shown in the following photographs:

Thumb rests on 4th string   Fingers slightly curved

Sometimes a technique of playing the strings from underneath is used, as illustrated in the photograph below:

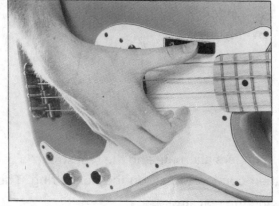

This is commonly used by 'funk' players to achieve a 'slapping' effect.

SECTION ONE

Section I introduces the student to basic music theory and notation, with special emphasis on reading music in the open position. The exercises are based upon common chord progressions used in rock/pop music, including 12 Bar Blues and turnarounds. This section provides the groundwork for the more advanced rhythms, techniques and theory discussed in the latter sections of the book.

STING (Courtesy Festival)

14

LESSON ONE

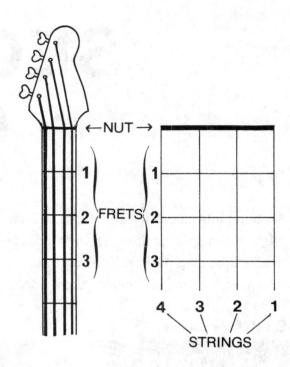

FRETBOARD DIAGRAM

A fretboard diagram is a grid pattern of strings (vertical lines) and frets (horizontal lines) which is used to indicate the position of notes.

OPEN STRING NOTES

The following fretboard diagram illustrates the four open string notes of the bass guitar.

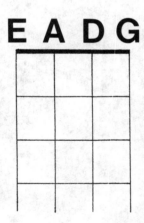

Here are the four notes in music and tablature notation.

Play each of these notes with a downward pick motion, indicated thus: **V**

EXERCISE ONE

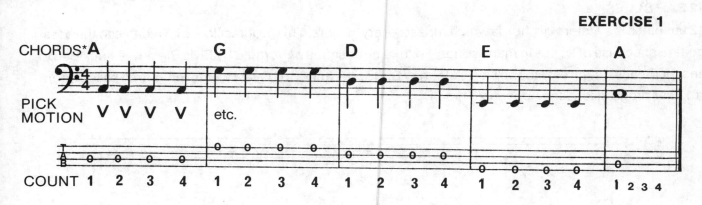

The two numbers immediately after the clef are referred to as the **time signature.** The time signature indicates the number of beats per bar (the top number) and the type of note receiving one beat (the bottom number).

4 — this number indicates four beats per bar.

4 — this number indicates that each beat is worth a quarter note.

4/4 is the most common time signature and is sometimes represented by this symbol called common time.

A **quarter note** (sometimes called a crotchet) ♩ has the value of one beat and four quarter notes are needed for one bar in 4/4 time, i.e. a quarter note is played on each beat.

In the last bar a **whole note** (or semibreve) ○ is used. The whole note is worth four counts and is played on the first beat and held for the remainder of the bar. It is equivalent to four quarter notes.

* Chords are played by a rhythm guitarist or keyboard player. **A** is a shorthand method of writing **A major.** It applies to all major chords.

LESSON TWO

12 BAR BLUES

12 bar blues is a pattern of chords which repeats every 12 bars. This progression is invaluable to the bass guitarist because of its use in many songs. For example, songs performed by Elvis Presley, Chuck Berry and the Beatles, such as "Hound Dog", "Johnny B. Goode" and "Roll Over Beethoven" are all based upon a 12 bar progression (see Appendix Three.)

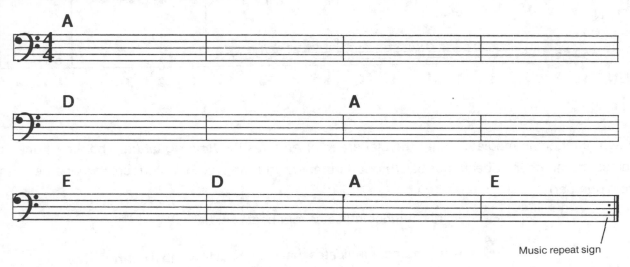

Music repeat sign

Music Repeat Sign: This indicates that the progression is repeated from the beginning. After the repeat, the progression finishes on the opening chord (in this case, an A chord). This practice will apply throughout the book.

LED ZEPPLIN (Courtesy WEA)

The following exercise (and Exercise 1) uses a **root note** bass for each chord. A root note is the note with the same name as the chord and will always blend well with that chord.

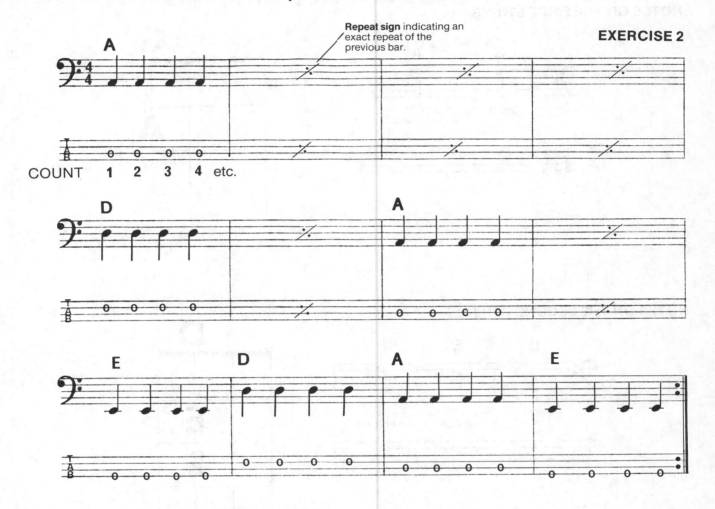

Finish the progression with an A note held for four counts.

THE POLICE

LESSON THREE

NOTES ON THE FIRST STRING

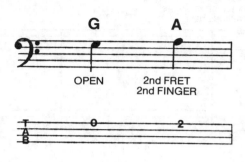

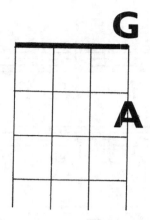

NOTES ON THE SECOND STRING

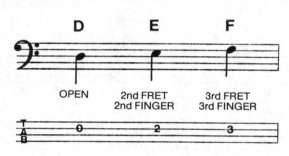

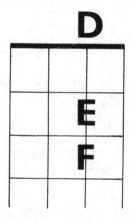

When playing notes the following rules should be observed:

1. Fingers on tips and directly behind frets.
2. Hold strings firmly against fretboard.
3. Use correct fingering (first finger — first fret, second finger — second fret, etc.).
4. Left hand fingers must remain close to the strings at all times; e.g. when an open string is played, your fingers should still be in close proximity.

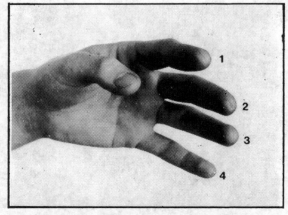

LEFT HAND FINGER NUMBERS

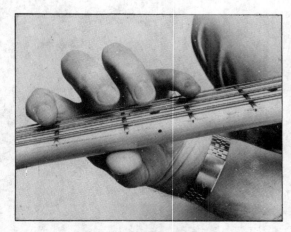

LEFT HAND POSITION

EXERCISES ON THE FIRST & SECOND STRINGS

The following exercise uses root notes throughout.

COUNT 1 2 3 4 etc.

Exercise Four uses the same chord progression with different bass notes. This is the first exercise that uses notes other than root notes.

COUNT 1 2 3 4 etc.

Remember that the progression finishes on an A minor chord and so you should finish on an A note (root note of the A minor chord).

* **Am** is a shorthand method for writing the **A minor** chord.

LESSON FOUR

THE HALF NOTE

♩ This is a **half note** (or minum) worth two counts. Two half notes make up a complete bar in ⁴⁄₄ time and are played on the first and third beats.

In the following exercise there are two chords per bar.

EXERCISE 5

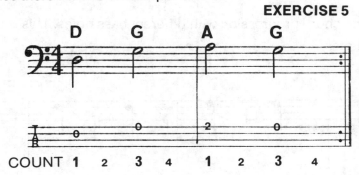

Here is a timing variation of the above exercise using half notes and quarter notes.

EXERCISE 6

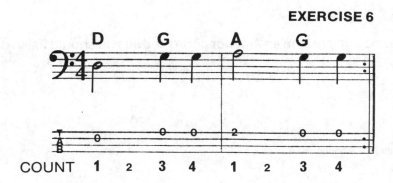

LESSON FIVE

NOTES ON THE THIRD STRING

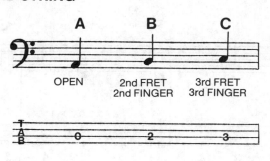

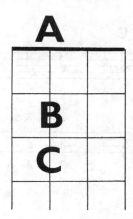

NOTES ON THE FOURTH STRING

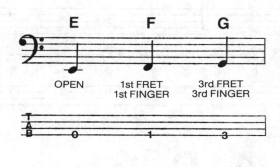

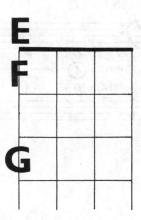

TURNAROUND PROGRESSION No. 1

The turnaround is another very important progression for you to become familiar with because, like 12 bar blues, it is the basis of many songs (see Appendix Three). The following turnaround is in the key of C major. The key of a song is generally indicated by the opening chord.

EXERCISE 7

Whereas Exercise 7 uses root notes and quarter note timing, Exercise 8 uses extra notes (other than root notes) and combines half and quarter notes.

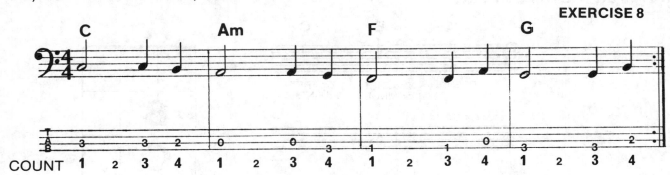

OPEN STRING NOTES

All the notes so far studied, as summarised in the diagram below, are in the **open position.** The open position consists of the open string notes and the notes on the first three frets.

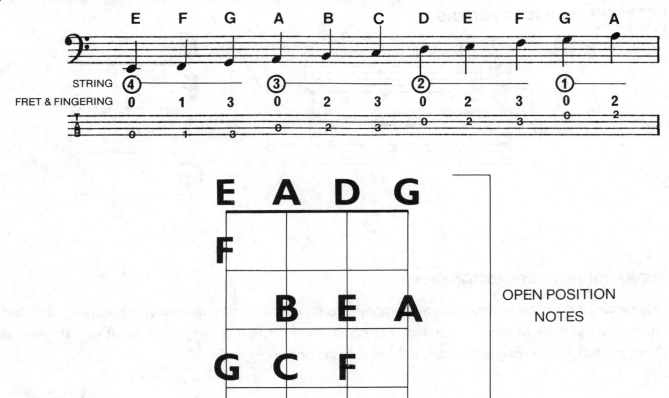

OPEN POSITION NOTES

By playing through the notes you will notice that B to C and E to F are only one fret apart (called a semitone), whereas all other notes are two frets apart (called a tone). The distance between notes of the musical alphabet can be set out as such:

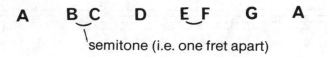

semitone (i.e. one fret apart)

It is essential for you to remember this pattern of notes.

LESSON SIX

TURNAROUND PROGRESSION No. 2

The chord progression used in turnaround two is very similar to that of turnaround one, except for the second chord (E minor in place of A minor). See Appendix Three for examples of songs using this turnaround.

EXERCISE 9

COUNT **1**   **2**   **3**   **4** etc.

The 4th bar of this exercise (G—F—E—D) features a **bass note run.** A bass note run is a group of notes which are used to connect chords together. Another example of a bass note run is in the last bar of Exercise Four (Lesson Three).

FIRST AND SECOND ENDINGS

The following turnaround progression uses first and second endings. On the first time through the progression, ending one is played (|¹   ), then the progression is repeated (as indicated by the repeat sign), and ending two is played (|²   ). Be careful not to play both endings together.

EXERCISE 10

COUNT **1**   **2**   **3**   **4** etc.

The second ending (G—F—E—D) features a **bass note run** leading back to the C note.

LESSON SEVEN

NOTES ON THE 4TH AND 5TH FRETS

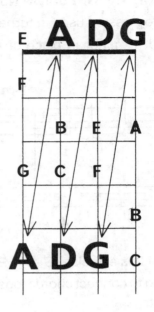

STRING	4	3	2	1	1
FRET	5	5	5	4	5

You will notice that the fretted A, D and G notes are the same as the open A, D and G notes introduced in Lesson One*. The B and C notes on the first string are notes you have not played before.

12 BAR IN C

The following blues introduces the quarter note rest, ⚬ , which indicates one beat of silence. This is achieved by releasing the pressure of the left hand fingers. The resulting sound is short and detached (called **staccato**), as compared to the smoother sound of two half notes (called **legato**). i.e.:

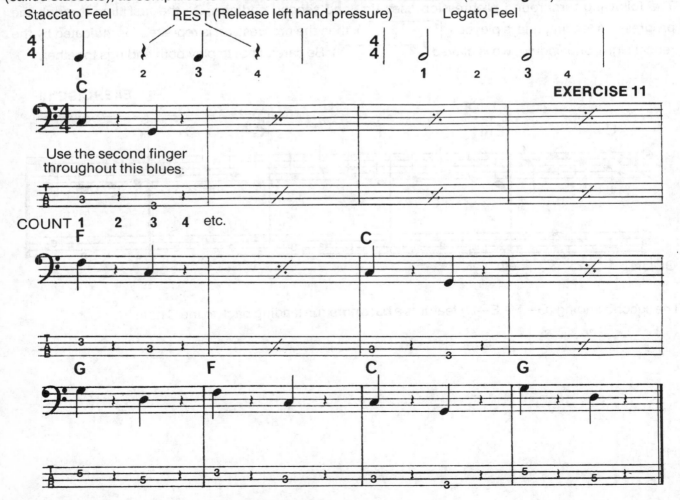

Use the second finger throughout this blues.

COUNT 1 2 3 4 etc.

EXERCISE 11

*These notes are used for tuning the bass guitar, as outlined in Appendix One.

Bass note runs can be added to this blues to make it more interesting. Use the first and second fingers.

EXERCISE 12

COUNT 1 2 3 4 1 2 3 4 etc.

QUEEN (Courtesy WEA)

LESSON EIGHT

THE MAJOR SCALE

The major scale is a series of eight notes in alphabetical order, based on a sequence of **tone-tone-semitone-tone-tone-tone-semitone.** This gives the familiar sound of **DO RA ME FA SO LA TE DO.** The name of the major scale is taken from its first note (called the root note). Here is the C major scale:

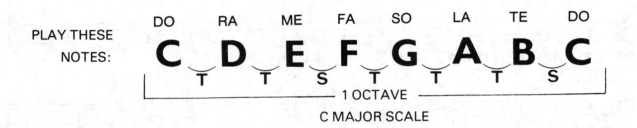

The C major scale can be written on the staff as such:

EXERCISE 13

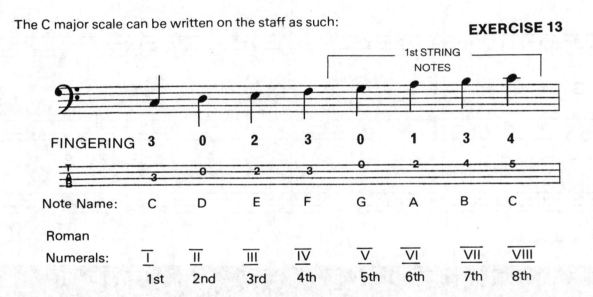

Each note of the scale can be identified by using Roman numerals. Thus F is said to be the 4th of the C scale, G is the 5th and so on.

¾ TIME

¾ time indicates three quarter note beats per bar. e.g.:

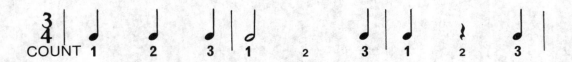

¾ time is often referred to as "Waltz Time".

The following exercise, which is in $\frac{3}{4}$ time, uses the C major scale as a descending bass line.

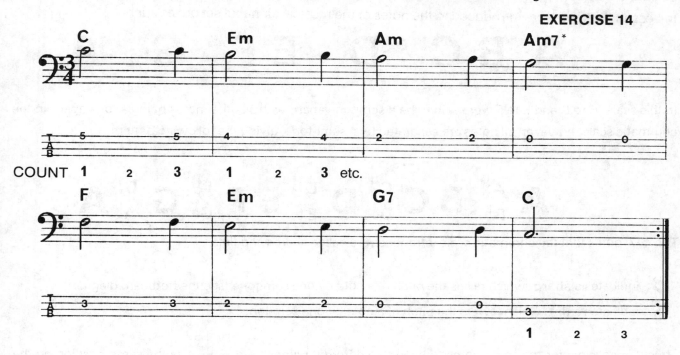

COUNT 1 2 3 1 2 3 etc.

The last bar of this progression uses a **dotted half note,** which is worth three counts. The dot is a sign placed after a note indicating that its time value is extended by a half. e.g.:

   = 2 counts   = 3 counts

   = 1 count   = 1½ counts

*Am7 is shorthand for A minor seventh.

LESSON NINE
SHARPS & FLATS

In Lesson Five you were introduced to the notes of the musical alphabet set out as such:

A B C D E F G A

In this scale, B to C and E to F were said to be a semitone apart, with all other notes being a tone apart. In the chromatic scale, however, all notes are separated by a semi-tone, giving the following pattern:

A A♯/B♭ B C C♯/D♭ D D♯/E♭ E F F♯/G♭ G G♯/A♭ A

The new notes that the chromatic scale introduces are called sharps and flats.

♯ indicates a **sharp,** which raises the pitch of a note by one semitone (see the fretboard diagram)

♭ indicates a **flat,** which lowers the pitch of a note by one semitone.

Thus it is possible for the same notes to have two different names. (e.g. F♯ has the same position on the fretboard as G♭). Below is a representation of the chromatic scale on the fretboard.

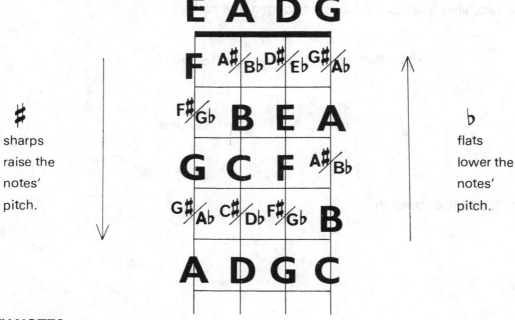

sharps raise the notes' pitch.

flats lower the notes' pitch.

EIGHTH NOTES

An eighth note (or quaver) ♪ is worth half a count. Two eighth notes, which are usually joined by a bar ♫, have the same value as a quarter note. Eighth notes are counted as such:

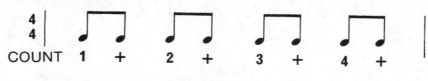

| COUNT | 1 | + | 2 | + | 3 | + | 4 | + |

Say aloud: One and   Two and   Three and   Four and

Here is a combination of half notes, quarter notes and eighth notes in $\frac{4}{4}$ time.

COUNT **1** **2 + 3 4 +** **1** 2 **3 + 4 +** **1** 2 **3** **4 +**

RIFFS

Bass guitarists often use a technique of playing "riffs" against a chord progression. A riff is a pattern of notes (usually for one or two bars duration) that is repeated throughout a progression (or song). The following riff uses eighth notes and has two sharps, C# and F#.

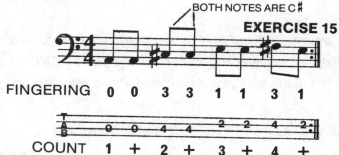

BOTH NOTES ARE C#

EXERCISE 15

In this riff both C notes are sharpened. This is because of the rule that a sharp (or flat), when placed before a note, affects the same note if it reoccurs in the remainder of that bar.

FINGERING **0 0 3 3 1 1 3 1**

COUNT **1 + 2 + 3 + 4 +**

For ease of playing, use the 1st and 3rd fingers as indicated, and when changing from E to F# leave the first finger down in preparation for the next E note. This riff can be applied to a 12 bar blues in A. Be sure to observe the above rule for playing sharps in each bar.

EXERCISE 16

COUNT **1 + 2 + 3 + 4 +** etc.

You have probably heard this riff style of playing before. Play some records (fifties rock and roll or blues songs would be best) and listen to the bass guitarist.

LESSON TEN

NOTES ON THE FRETBOARD

The following fretboard diagram outlines all the **natural** notes (i.e. no sharps or flats) up to the 12th fret.

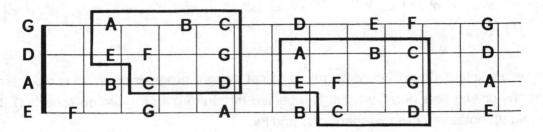

In Lesson Eight you were introduced to the C major scale which consists of the notes C D E F G A B C. This scale can be played as a pattern on the fretboard, commencing on either the 3rd fret of the 3rd string or the 8th fret of the 4th string as outlined above. Play through this pattern using the fingering as indicated.

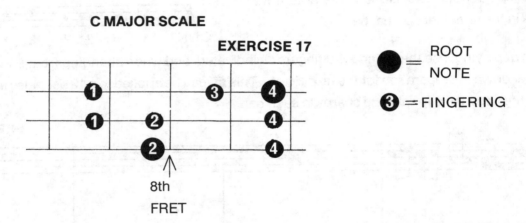

This pattern can be moved to different positions and still retain the major scale sound (DO RA ME etc.). For example, the A major scale commences on the A note at the 5th fret of the 4th string.

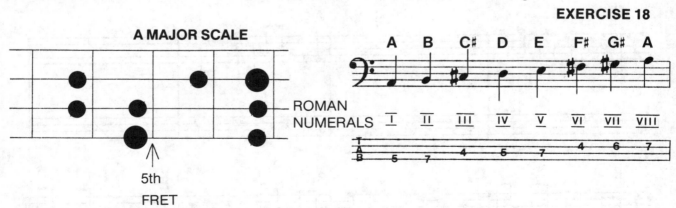

In keeping with the major scale sequence of tone-tone-semitone-tone-tone-tone-semitone, the A major scale contains C#, F#, and G# notes. This same scale/pattern can be played commencing on the A note at the 12th fret of the 3rd string, all notes being one octave higher.

The major scale pattern can be played by starting at any note on the 3rd or 4th string. The note you start on will be the root note of the scale. For example, if you start on the E♭ note at the 6th fret of the 3rd string you will be playing the E♭ major scale:

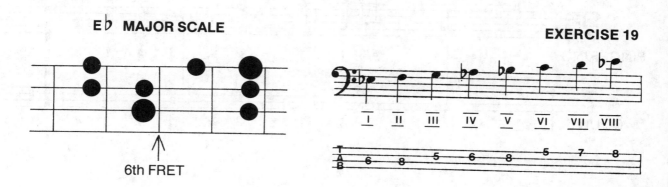

E♭ MAJOR SCALE

EXERCISE 19

6th FRET

This major scale can also be played at the 11th fret of the 4th string.

A summary of major scales is given in Appendix Two.

HIGHER POSITION EXERCISES

The following exercises use notes in the higher positions. Music readers should refer to the tablature for the string location of each note.

EXERCISE 20A

12 BAR IN A

FINGERING   0   0   3   0   3   0   3   1   etc.

COUNT   **1** + **2** + **3** + **4** + etc.

NOTE READING EXERCISES

The following well-known melodies have been included for extra note reading practice. Remember that these are note reading exercises only, and that a bass player **does not** usually play the melody of a song (he plays an accompaniment to the melody.)

AURA LEE

MORNING HAS BROKEN

SONG OF JOY

SECTION $\bar{I}$ SUMMARY

You have now completed the first section of this book, and written below is a summary of what has been studied. You should revise the contents of the list thoroughly, before commencing to Section $\bar{II}$.

NOTATION: Music Notation
> Tablature notation
> Open position notes
> Higher position notes
> Sharps and Flats

NOTE VALUES: As summarised in the following table (including rests).

WHOLE NOTE	HALF NOTE	QUARTER NOTE	EIGHTH NOTE
4 (COUNTS)	2	1	½

WHOLE NOTE REST	HALF NOTE REST	QUARTER NOTE REST	EIGHTH NOTE REST

MUSIC THEORY: Basic musical terms (i.e. staff, bass clef, bar, bar line, double bar line, etc.)
> Time signatures: $\frac{4}{4}$ and $\frac{3}{4}$
> Root note
> Bass note runs
> First and second endings
> Staccato and legato
> Riffs
> Major scale

BASIC PROGRESSIONS: 12 bar blues
> Turnaround one, turnaround two

Also read Appendices One and Three.

SECTION TWO

Section $\overline{\text{II}}$ introduces the student to riff playing. All of the important scales and techniques used by bass guitarists are discussed, including major, minor and blues scales in positions over the entire fretboard. The exercises gradually introduce more complex timing variations, including specialized rock and reggae rhythms.

Upon completion of this section the student will have gained the knowledge and practical ability to play in a group.

POLICE (Courtesy Festival)

LESSON ELEVEN

THE 12 BAR BLUES PROGRESSION

In Lesson Two you were introduced to the 12 bar blues progression as outlined below.

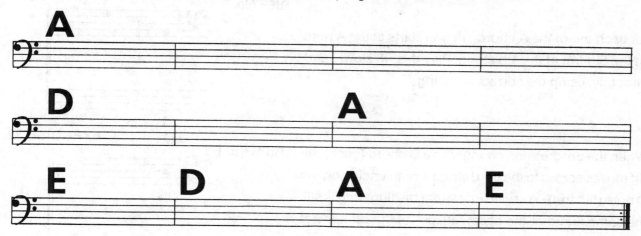

Underneath each chord roman numerals (as introduced in Lesson Eight) have been written to indicate the basic chords used in 12 bar progressions. It is important for you to remember that 12 bar blues in any key uses the 3 chords, $\overline{I}$, $\overline{IV}$ and $\overline{V}$ in the following sequence:

$$
\begin{array}{|c|c|c|c|}
\hline
\overline{I} & & & \\
\hline
\overline{IV} & & \overline{I} & \\
\hline
\overline{V} & \overline{IV} & \overline{I} & \overline{V} \; :\| \\
\hline
\end{array}
$$

For example, in the key of C the $\overline{I}$, $\overline{IV}$ and $\overline{V}$ chords are C, F and G respectively. In the key of G the $\overline{I}$, $\overline{IV}$ and $\overline{V}$ chords are G, C and D.

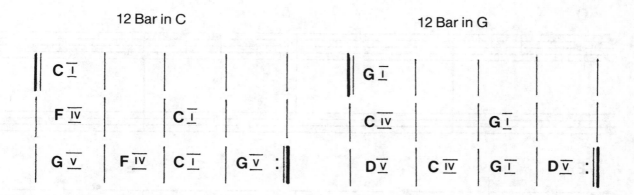

See Appendix Three for a list of songs which use the 12 bar blues progression.

12 BAR RIFF No. 1

In Lesson Nine you were introduced to the style of playing riffs over a chord progression. The following example, riff one, is played against the 12 bar blues in the key of A.

RIFF No. 1

A   **EXERCISE 21**

For each bar of the A chord, riff one starts at the A note on the 5th fret of the 4th string. Play this riff slowly and smoothly, using the correct fingering.

RIFF No. 1

D   **EXERCISE 22**

When the progression changes to a D chord (bar 5) the riff moves across to the third string, commencing on the D note (5th fret). You will notice that the fingering is still the same and that the basic "shape" of the riff has not altered.

RIFF No. 1

E   **EXERCISE 23**

For the E chord (bar 9), the riff shape begins on the 3rd string at the 7th fret. Once again, the fingering and basic riff shape remain the same.

Here is the complete 12 bar in A.

RIFF No. 1   **A**

EXERCISE 24

LESSON TWELVE

RIFF VARIATIONS

Variations to a basic riff can be achieved by changing the sequence and/or timing of the notes. For example, riff one could be varied as such:

Variation One — altering the note sequence.

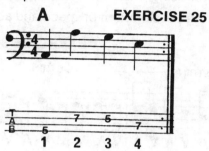

Variation Two — altering the timing.

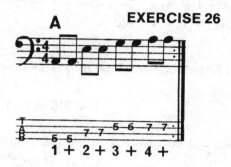

Variation Three — altering the sequence and timing.

Play each of these variations against the 12 bar in A. Experiment with some of your own combinations.

LESSON THIRTEEN

ALTERNATE PICKING

All previous exercises have involved playing the notes with a downward motion of the pick, which is represented thus: **V**

In the exercises below, the technique of using down and up (**∧**) picking is introduced. This is called **alternate picking,** and it is essential for the development of speed and accuracy.

EXERCISE 30

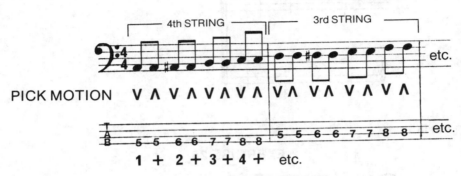

Continue on through the second and first strings and then play back down to the fourth string.

EXERCISE 31

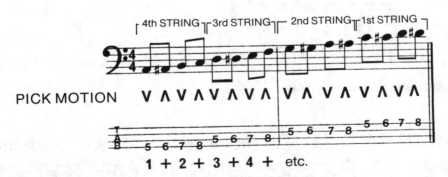

The pattern of notes that you are playing in these exercises will look like this on the fretboard diagram:

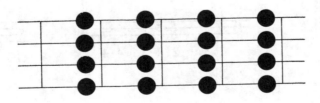

This is purely an exercise to "loosen up" your fingers and should be practised every day in all positions on the fretboard (e.g. starting at the first fret and working through to the 12th fret etc.).

RIFF TWO

The following riff uses alternate picking and involves notes of the A major scale.

Here is riff 2 in the 12 bar blues progression.

LESSON FOURTEEN

TRANSPOSING

As a competent bass guitarist you will need to be able to play the 12 bar blues progression in any key. The process of changing keys is called **transposition.**

The following riff is in the key of G:

This riff commences on the G note (to match the G chord). When the chord changes to C and D the riff position will change accordingly (starting on the C and D notes respectively).

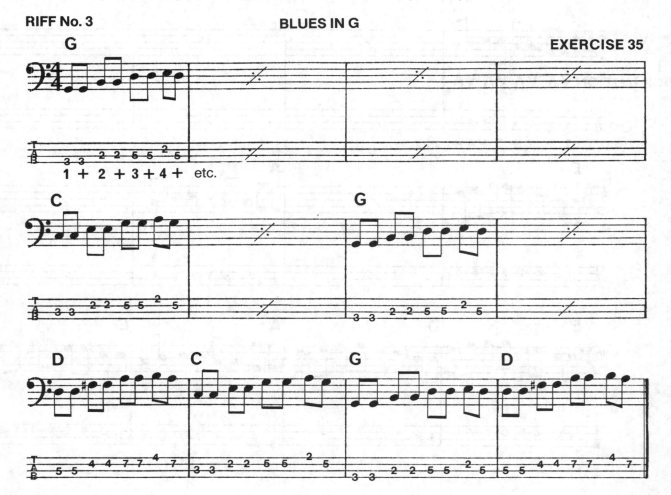

If you wish to transpose this riff into the key of A (using the A(I̅), D(I̅V̅) and E(V̅) chords), commence the riff on the A note (5th fret of the 4th string) and change to the D and E sections accordingly.

To transpose the riff into the key of C (using the C(I̅), F(I̅V̅) and G(V̅) chords), commence the riff on the C note at the 8th fret of the 4th string. For the F chord, commence on the 8th fret of the 3rd string and for the G chord commence on the 10th fret of the 3rd string.

12 BAR BLUES PATTERN ONE

If you play through the three 12 bar blues examples given in this lesson you will see a pattern being formed. This pattern, illustrated below, represents the commencing note for each riff of the 3 chords in the 12 bar blues.

BLUES PATTERN ONE

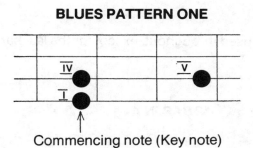

Commencing note (Key note)

The **key note** is the note with the same name as the key of the blues, e.g. for a blues in the key of A, A is the key note.

This 12 bar blues pattern can be played by commencing on any fret of the 4th string. The note you start on will be the key note, indicating the key of the blues, e.g. If you start at the 6th fret, a B♭ note, you will be playing a blues in the key of B♭.

The pattern can also be played on a 3rd string note, as such:

BLUES PATTERN ONE

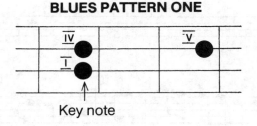

Key note

This variation is more convenient for keys such as E i.e. commencing on the 7th fret of the 3rd string rather than the 12th fret of the 4th string.

Using blues pattern one you can now play a 12 bar blues in any key.

44

LESSON FIFTEEN

RIFF No. 4

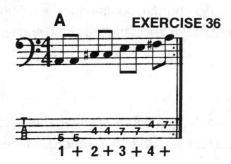

In the following 12 bar blues, riff 4 is used throughout, except for the last bar. This last bar makes use of a very common ending for blues riffs.

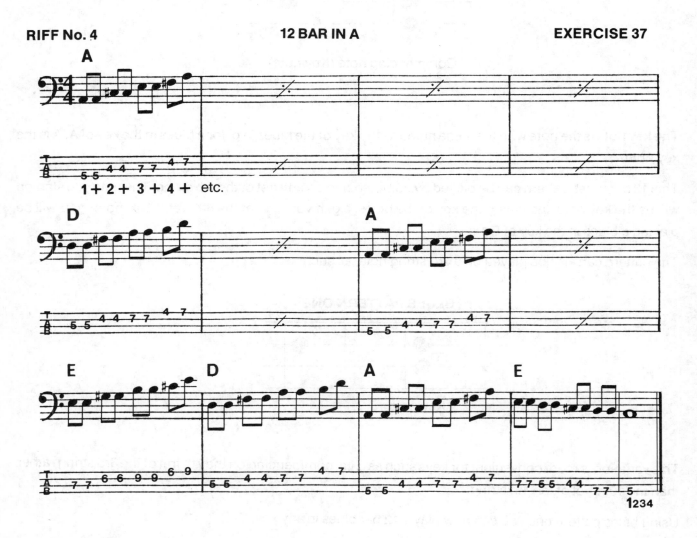

Transpose this riff into other keys, as discussed in the previous lesson.

LESSON SIXTEEN

RIFF No. 5

Riff 5 is a two bar riff, and is used in the first 8 bars of the 12 bar progression. In bars 9 and 10 riff 2 is used (a one bar riff to match one bar of each chord) and in bars 11 and 12 a new ending is introduced.

RIFF No. 5   **EXERCISE 38**

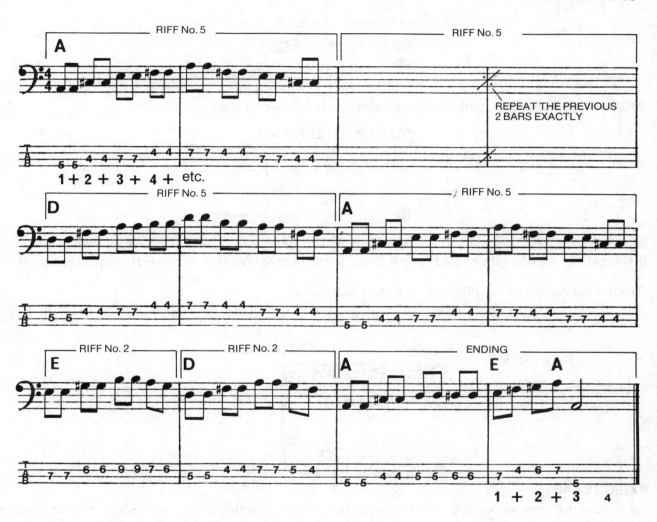

LESSON SEVENTEEN

12 BAR BLUES PATTERN TWO

In Lesson Fourteen you were introduced to a pattern on the fretboard which enabled you to play 12 bar blues in any key (by transposing). This pattern involved the $\overline{\text{I}}$, $\overline{\text{IV}}$ and $\overline{\text{V}}$ starting notes being played on the 4th and 3rd strings as such:

BLUES PATTERN ONE

Another commonly used pattern commences on the following notes:

BLUES PATTERN TWO

In this pattern the riff notes of the $\overline{\text{IV}}$ and $\overline{\text{V}}$ chord are an octave lower than if played using blues pattern one.

Play the following half bar riff (i.e. play it twice each bar):

RIFF No. 6

EXERCISE 40

For a blues in D commence at the 5th fret of the 3rd string for the D($\overline{\text{I}}$) chord, the 3rd fret of the 4th string for the G($\overline{\text{IV}}$) chord, and at the 5th fret of the 4th string for the A($\overline{\text{V}}$) chord.

LESSON EIGHTEEN

12 BAR BLUES PATTERN THREE

For riffs which involve playing notes on all four strings a new pattern must be used. In this pattern each riff position commences on the 4th string, as illustrated below:

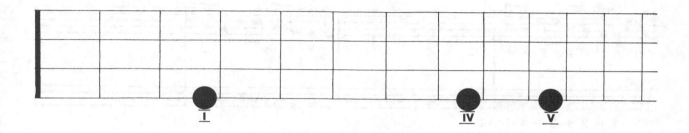

Try the following riff.

RIFF No. 7   **EXERCISE 41**

EXERCISE 42

Play this riff as a 12 bar in G, commencing at the 3rd fret for the G(Ī) chord, the 8th fret for the C(ĪV) chord and the 10th fret for the D(V̄) chord.

VAN HALEN

LESSON NINETEEN

RIFF No. 8

Riffs can be played against virtually any chord progression (i.e. not just 12 bar blues). The following example illustrates a one bar riff played against the Am, Gm and Fm chords.

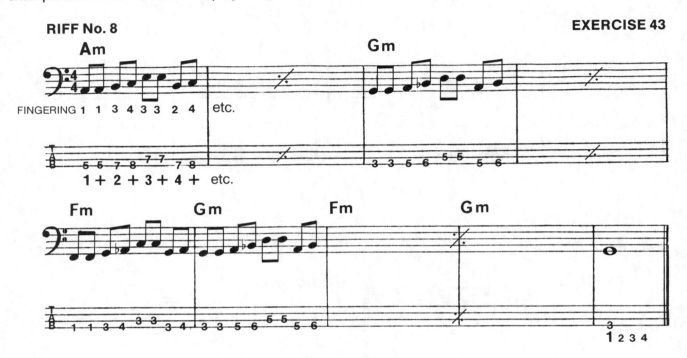

RIFF No. 8   **EXERCISE 43**

This riff uses notes from a minor scale, because it is played against minor chords. Minor scales are discussed in more detail in Lesson Twenty Nine and in Appendix Two.

To maintain a smooth sound in this riff, use the fingering as indicated and use alternate picking.

Z.Z. TOP

LESSON TWENTY

RIFF No. 9

Riff 9 involves the use of **lead-In** notes which are notes that are played before the first bar of music. The riff commences on the second half of the third beat. as indicated by the count.

RIFF No. 9   **EXERCISE 44**

The above 12 bar blues finishes with 2 bars of an A chord, rather than returning to the E chord in the last bar. This is a common variation of 12 bar blues.

LESSON TWENTY ONE

TURNAROUND PATTERN ONE

In Lesson Five you were introduced to turnaround one in the key of C, using the C(I), Am(VIm), F(IV) and G(V) chords. Written below is the same turnaround in the key of A.

If you play through this turnaround using the root notes of each chord on the 4th and 3rd strings, the following pattern is established:

Turnaround Pattern One — Key of A

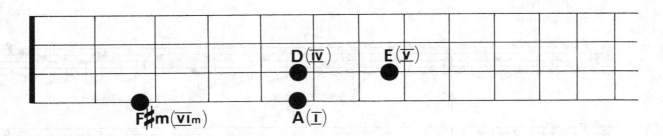

As with the 12 bar blues, this pattern can be transposed to other keys. For example, try a turnaround in C:

Turnaround Pattern One — Key of C

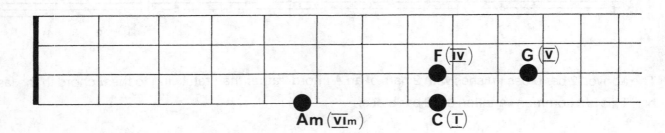

DOTTED QUARTER NOTES

In Lesson Eight you were introduced to the dotted quarter note (worth 1½ counts) which is used in the following exercise. This is a very common bass rhythm.

Play this rhythm (using root notes) with turnaround one in the key of A.

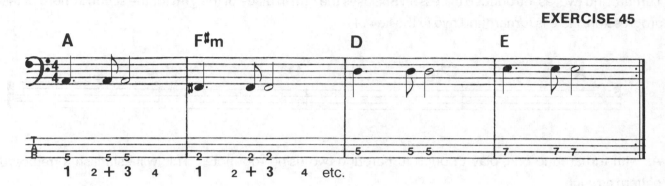

Here is a variation to the above rhythm:

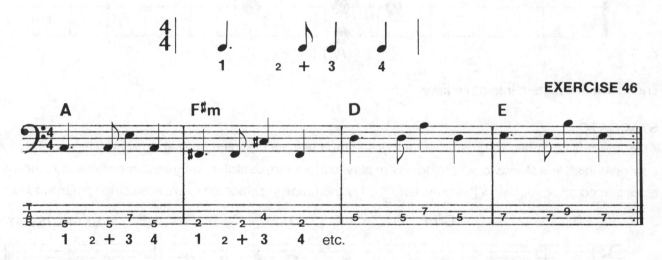

ROXY MUSIC (Courtesy Polygram)

LESSON TWENTY TWO

TURNAROUND PATTERN No. TWO

Turnaround two, as introduced in Lesson Six, uses the $\overline{\text{III}}$m in place of the $\overline{\text{VI}}$m for the second chord of the progression. Here is turnaround two in the key of A.

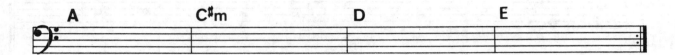

As with turnaround one, play through turnaround two using root notes. This will establish a fretboard pattern as such:

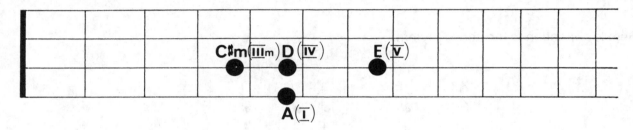

Transpose this pattern into other keys.

STACCATO

All of the riffs you have so far studied in this section have been played in a legato style (i.e. smoothly). A contrasting style is **staccato**, where notes are played in a short, detached manner. Staccato is indicated by a dot placed above or below the note. i.e. ♩ Try the following staccato exercises using turnaround two.

Exercise 48 uses the same rhythm as in Exercise 46, but is played in a staccato fashion.

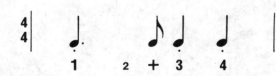

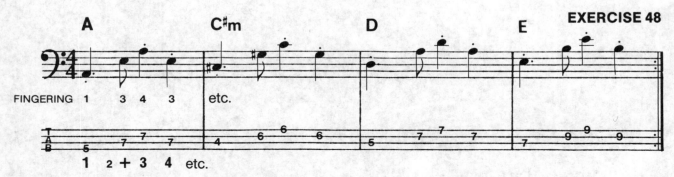

LESSON TWENTY THREE

THE TIE

In music, the tie is a curved line joining two (or more) notes of the same pitch, where the second note(s) is not played, but its time value is added to that of the first note.

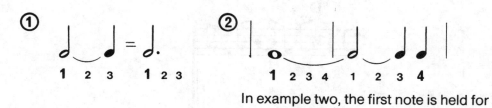

In example two, the first note is held for seven counts.

A tie is necessary if a note is played over a bar line, as in example two above and in the 2 bar riff below.

RIFF No. 10   **EXERCISE 49**

In tablature notation the curved line of a tie is not necessary.

You will notice that in this riff all notes are lower in pitch than the starting note (root note). This is unlike all previous riffs where notes have all been above the starting note.

RIFF No. 11   EXERCISE 50

Riff 11 uses a tie within the bar.

EXERCISE 51

Play this riff as a 12 bar blues in D, against the chords D(Ī), G(ĪV) and A(V̄). Use 12 bar blues pattern one commencing on the 5th fret of the 3rd string.

LESSON TWENTY FOUR

EIGHTH NOTE REST

In the previous lesson (Exercise Fifty) you were introduced to a tie on the 3rd beat of the bar as such:

RIFF No. 11   **EXERCISE 50**

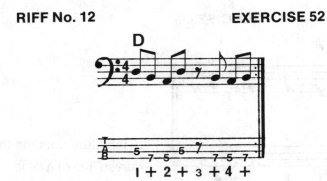

A staccato feel can be created by using an eighth note rest, ⁊ , on the 3rd beat.

RIFF No. 12   **EXERCISE 52**

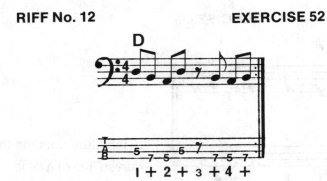

The eighth note rest indicates half a beat of silence, which, in the above example occurs on the 3rd beat.

The rest is achieved by releasing pressure on the left hand (as with staccato).

In the two bar riff below (riff 13) the eighth note rest is used on the first count of the second bar.

RIFF No. 13   **EXERCISE 53**

Here is another two bar riff combining the 8th note rest and the tie.

RIFF No. 14   **EXERCISE 54**

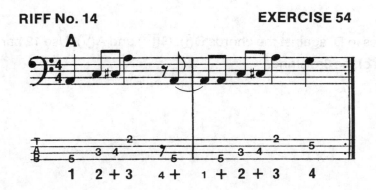

LESSON TWENTY FIVE

TRIPLET TIMING

In triplet timing, three evenly spaced notes are played in each beat (indicated thus 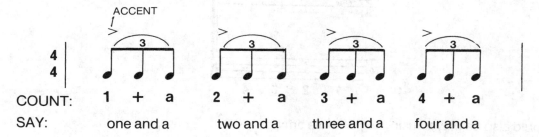). They should be played with an accent on the first note of each group of three (i.e. accent each note that falls "on" the beat). Triplets create a fast waltz feel.

Try the following turnaround exercise using triplets.

EXERCISE 55

In the above turnaround each chord is played for only 2 beats (as compared to 4 beats in all previous turnarounds). It is important to remember that in turnaround progressions the order of the chords must not change, but the duration of each chord (i.e. the number of beats) may vary.

TRIPLET RIFF

The following progression, although not a 12 bar pattern, has a blues feel.

RIFF No. 15   **EXERCISE 56**

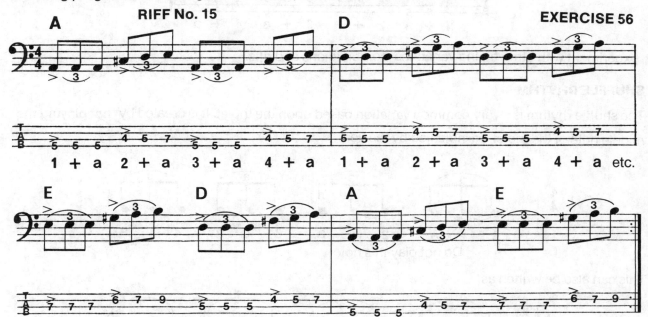

* In music, these are referred to as eighth note triplets (see the Glossary of Musical Terms).

LESSON TWENTY SIX

RHYTHM VARIATIONS

In Lesson Twelve you were introduced to the following riff, using quarter note timing:

This riff could also be played using eighth note timing:

or triplet timing:

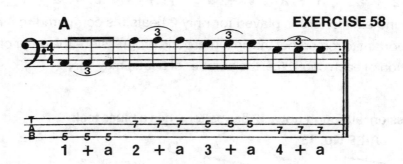

experiment with other timing variations, combinations and riffs.

SHUFFLE RHYTHM

The shuffle rhythm is a very common variation based upon the triplet. It is created by **not playing** the middle note of the triplet, as indicated by the tie.

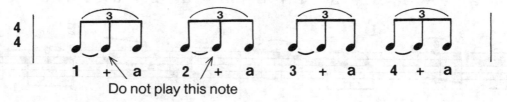

This can also be written as:

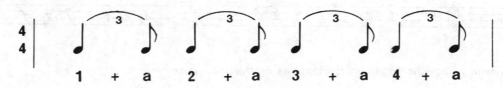

Exercise 58, played as a shuffle, becomes:

EXERCISE 59

EXERCISE 60. Play this riff as a 12 bar in A.

A staccato feel can be achieved by playing a rest on the middle count of the triplet, as such:

Release left hand pressure to achieve rest

8 BAR BLUES

Although 12 bar is the most common structure for blues, an 8 bar pattern can also be used, as illustrated below. The staccato shuffle is used throughout.

8 BAR BLUES

EXERCISE 62

LESSON TWENTY SEVEN

THE BLUES SCALE

In Lesson Eight you were introduced to the major scale. Another useful scale used by bass guitarists is the blues scale, which consists of the $\underline{I}, \underline{III}\flat, \underline{IV}, \underline{V}$ and $\underline{VII}\flat$ notes of the major scale. Thus the A blues scale is derived:

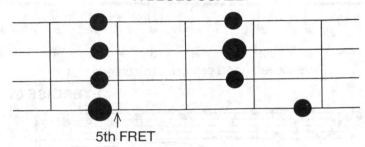

	A	B	C♯	D	E	F♯	G♯	A
A major scale:	$\underline{I}$	$\underline{II}$	$\underline{III}$	$\underline{IV}$	$\underline{V}$	$\underline{VI}$	$\underline{VII}$	$\underline{VIII}$

	A	C	D	E	G	A
A blues scale:	$\underline{I}$	$\underline{III}\flat$	$\underline{IV}$	$\underline{V}$	$\underline{VII}\flat$	$\underline{VIII}$

These notes can be arranged into the following fretboard pattern.*

A BLUES SCALE

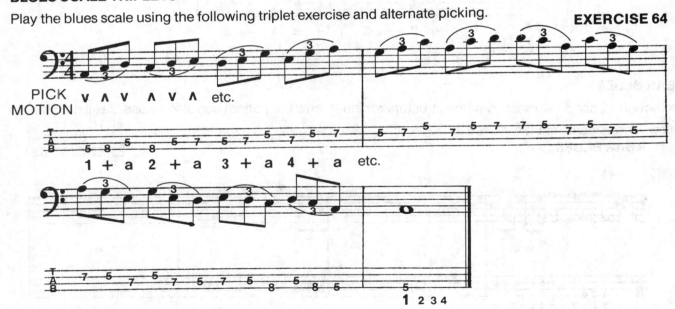

5th FRET

EXERCISE 63

Play through and memorize this pattern.

BLUES SCALE TRIPLETS

Play the blues scale using the following triplet exercise and alternate picking.

EXERCISE 64

PICK MOTION V ∧ V ∧ V ∧ etc.

1 + a   2 + a   3 + a   4 + a   etc.

1 2 3 4

BLUES SCALE OVER ENTIRE FRETBOARD

Exercise 64 is one of many which can be created by using blues scale notes. Here are the five notes of the A blues scale over the entire fretboard.

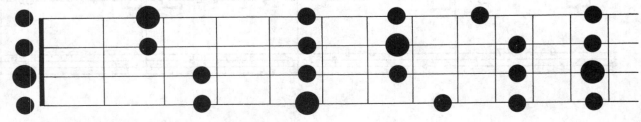

* $\underline{III}\flat$ indicates that the third note of the scale is flattened.

LESSON TWENTY EIGHT

RIFF/SCALE RELATIONSHIPS

The two scales you have so far studied are the major and blues scales. The table below lists the riffs studied in this section and the scale from which they were derived.

RIFF	BLUES	MAJOR	OTHER	
1	X			
2		X		
3		X		
4		X		
5		X		
6		X		
7			X	G9 arpeggio (discussed on page 83)
8			X	A minor "pure" scale (discussed in Lesson 28)
9			X	Major scale with a blues note (VIIb) added.
10		X		
11		X		
12		X		
13		X		
14			X	Blues scale with an additional note (C#)
15		X		

TRIPLET BLUES RIFF

The following two bar riff combines the staccato shuffle rhythm (on the first beat) with triplets.

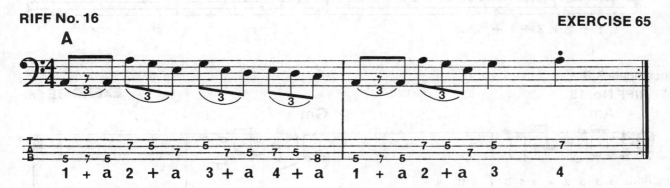

RIFF No. 16

EXERCISE 65

EXERCISE 66

Play this riff against a 12 bar in A. In bars 9 and 10 (the E and D chords) only the first bar of the riff is played, to fit in with the chord sequence.

LESSON TWENTY NINE

MINOR CHORD RIFFS

Riffs played against minor chords will use notes from the minor scales as discussed in Appendix Two. The main feature of all these scales in the flattened third note ($\flat III$) i.e. C natural in an A minor scale as compared to C sharp in an A major scale. Because the flattened third is also present in a blues scale, it is possible to use the blues scale to construct minor chord riffs. All of the notes of the blues scale are a part of the pure minor scale.

Pure Minor Scale Riff

An example of a riff using pure minor scale notes was given in Lesson Seventeen (Riff 8). This riff uses notes from the A minor pure scale against the Am chord, the G minor pure scale against the Gm chord and the F minor pure scale against the Fm chord.

Harmonic Minor Scale Riff

The following riff features a G# note which indicates that an A harmonic minor scale is being used. Observe the fingering.

RIFF No. 17   **EXERCISE 67**

Blues Scale Riff

RIFF No. 18   **EXERCISE 68**

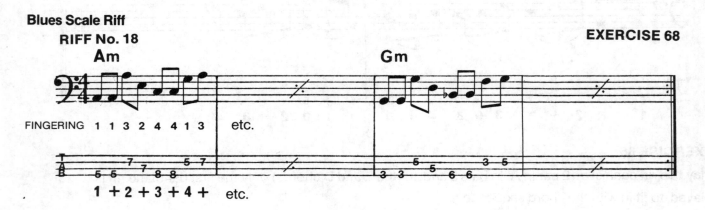

LESSON THIRTY

OCTAVES

A common "funk" style of playing involves the use of octave notes, e.g. instead of playing this:

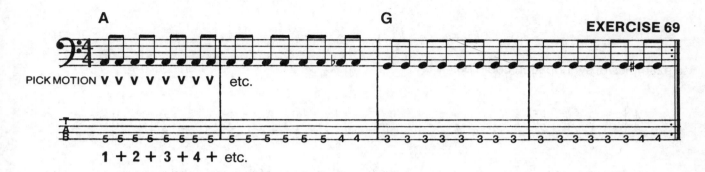

play this:

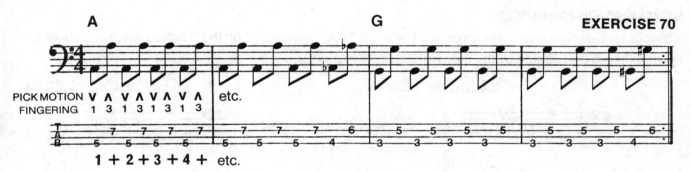

To avoid the notes overlapping (i.e. both octave notes sounding together) be sure to play each note for only its eighth note value. This can only be achieved by releasing pressure of the left hand fingers after each note is played, resulting in a "see-saw" motion of the first and third fingers.

Here is turnaround two using octaves.

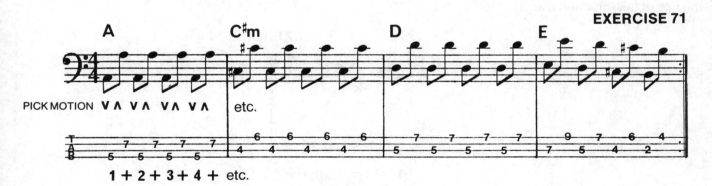

LESSON THIRTY ONE

SYNCOPATION

Syncopation can be defined as the placing of an accent on a normally unaccented beat, e.g. in $\frac{4}{4}$ time the normal accent is on the first and third beats:

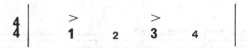

so examples of syncopation could be:

The accent can be achieved by merely playing louder or by the use of ties, rests and staccato notes. The exercise in Lessons Twenty Three and Twenty Four were examples of syncopation.

SYNCOPATION EXERCISES

The following exercise uses octave notes. The accent has been placed on the "and" count of each beat and syncopation is highlighted by the use of eighth note rests.

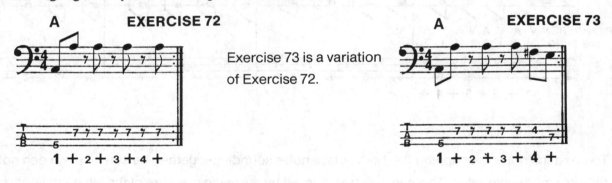

Exercise 73 is a variation of Exercise 72.

The timing of the following exercise is the same as that of Exercise 72, but the syncopation is achieved by the use of ties, creating a legato feel.

In this exercise the see-saw movement of the left hand, as discussed in the previous lesson, must be used.

LESSON THIRTY TWO

SYNCOPATED RHYTHM STYLES

Different styles of bass playing (e.g. reggae, bossa nova, etc.) use a distinctive syncopated rhythm, examples of which are illustrated below.

REGGAE Example 1

EXERCISE 76

Example 2

EXERCISE 77

BOSSA NOVA

EXERCISE 78

SAMBA

EXERCISE 79

MAMBO

EXERCISE 80

CHA-CHA

EXERCISE 81

LESSON THIRTY THREE

PASSING NOTES

All of the riffs you have so far played have been based on scales (i.e. major, minor and blues scales). Many riffs, however, use notes which are in between the given scale notes. These notes are referred to as passing notes.

The use of passing notes will create **chromatic runs,** i.e. moving one fret at a time. The following examples illustrate chromatic movement.

RIFF No. 19   **EXERCISE 82**

Play this riff as a 12 bar blues in A.

RIFF No. 20   **EXERCISE 83**

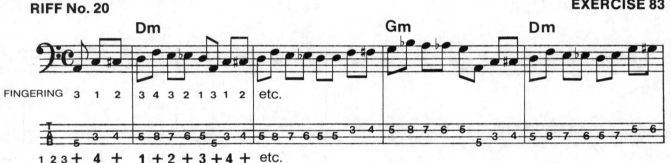

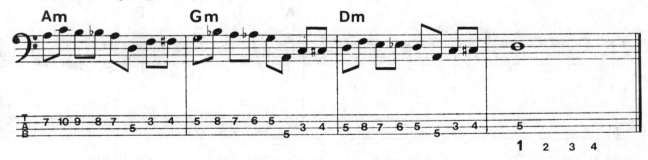

The following minor riff uses the blues scale notes (see Lesson Twenty Seven) with a G# passing note.

RIFF No. 21   **EXERCISE 84**

* D♯ and E♭ are **enharmonic** notes, as they have the same pitch (i.e. the same position on the fretboard) but are named differently. When a chromatic run is ascending, sharps are used and when descending, flats are used.

LESSON THIRTY FOUR

WALKING BASS

Walking bass is a style of playing which involves the use of scale notes and passing notes to create a more flowing bass line. Walking bass often features the use of quarter notes and creates a smoother connection between chords. It avoids the repetitious riff style of playing.

Here is a 12 bar blues in A using a walking bass style.

EXERCISE 85

LESSON THIRTY FIVE

WALKING BASS EXERCISES

The following walking bass examples illustrate the use of this style in rock and jazz progressions.

LESSON THIRTY SIX

SIXTEENTH NOTES

In music notation, a sixteenth note (or semiquaver) has the value of half an eighth note and is written as such:

Thus two sixteenth notes equal an eighth note, and four sixteenth notes equal a quarter note.

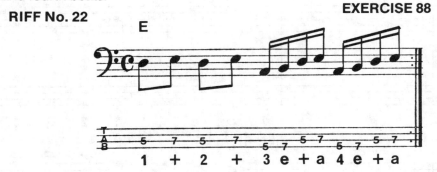

1 e + a

SAY "one e and a"

The syllables "1 e + a" are used to represent the sixteenth note count. Here is a riff using sixteenth notes on the third and fourth beats.

RIFF No. 22   **EXERCISE 88**

1 + 2 + 3 e + a 4 e + a

THE HAMMER ON

A "hammer on" refers to the technique of sounding a note without actually picking the string with the pick. The sound is produced by striking the string with one of the left hand fingers.

In the exercise below, only the D note is picked, and the third finger "hammers on" firmly to produce the sound of the E note.

EXERCISE 89

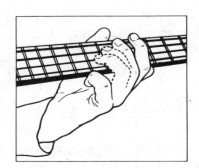

The hammer on effect is indicated by the curved line, and the small 'H' between the two notes in question. Remember that the second note (E), is not picked; the sound is produced entirely by the second finger 'hammering on' to the string.

You must be very careful with the timing of the hammer on. Both the D and E notes are eighth notes and each should have an equal time value when played (regardless of the hammer on technique).

Play riff 22 using hammer ons as indicated.

EXERCISE 90

To create a different feel with the hammer on it can be played faster. Compare the following:

Slow Hammer On

Quick Hammer On

In this example the E note is played immediately after the D note.

If the quick hammer on is applied to the first two beats of riff 22 it is written as such:

EXERCISE 91

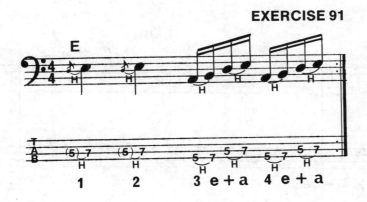

LESSON THIRTY SEVEN

THE SLIDE

The slide is a technique which involves a finger moving along the string to its new note. The finger maintains pressure on the string, so that a continuous sound is produced.

In the following turnaround the sliding technique is used between the "and" of the second beat and the third beat. Pick the E note and slide to F#. **Do not pick the F# note.**

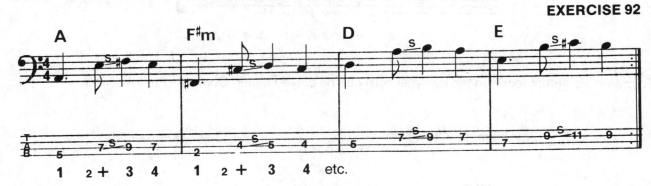

As with the hammer-on technique, a quick slide can also be played, when the second note is played immediately after the first. The quick slide is written as such:

RIFF No. 23

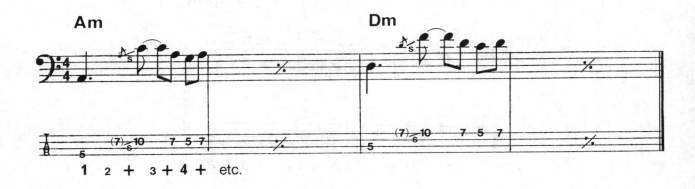

LESSON THIRTY EIGHT

TIMING COMBINATIONS

So far you have studied the following timing values.

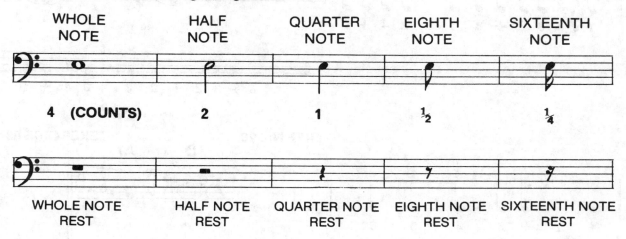

WHOLE NOTE	HALF NOTE	QUARTER NOTE	EIGHTH NOTE	SIXTEENTH NOTE
4 (COUNTS)	2	1	$\frac{1}{2}$	$\frac{1}{4}$

WHOLE NOTE REST	HALF NOTE REST	QUARTER NOTE REST	EIGHTH NOTE REST	SIXTEENTH NOTE REST

In addition to this table, you have also studied dotted notes and triplets. You should practice playing any combination of these notes. Try the following exercises and riffs.

RIFF No. 24   EXERCISE 94

RIFF No. 25   EXERCISE 95

RIFF No. 26   EXERCISE 96

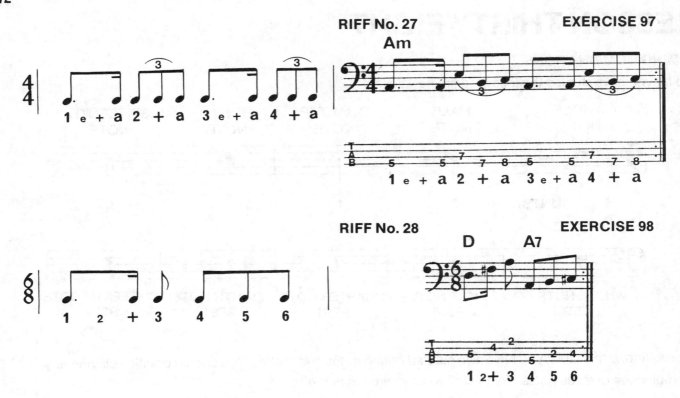

RIFF No. 27   **EXERCISE 97**

RIFF No. 28   **EXERCISE 98**

Riff No. 28 introduces $\frac{6}{8}$ time. $\frac{6}{8}$ time indicates 2 dotted quarter note beats per bar, which can be divided into 2 groups of eighth notes as such:

$\frac{6}{8}$ is an example of compound time because the beat is a dotted note.

FLEETWOOD MAC (Courtesy WEA)

Written below are some more timing variations. Use these timing values to create your own riffs.

SECTION II SUMMARY

In Section II you have covered the scales, rhythms and techniques used by all bass guitarists. If your ambition is to join a group, now is the time to do so. The only way to become a good bass guitarist is to gain the experience of playing with other musicians, which will improve your playing immensely.

As well as being in a group, you need to listen and copy other bass guitarists. Try to see as many live groups as possible.

Written below is a summary of what has been covered in Section II.

MUSIC THEORY: Roman numerals
Transposing
Lead-in notes
Blues scale
Riff/scale relationships
Minor scales
Syncopation
Passing notes
Position playing

NOTE VALUES: Dotted notes
Rests
Triplets
Shuffle
16th notes

EXERCISES AND
TECHNIQUES: 12 bar and turnaround patterns
Octaves
Walking bass
Alternate picking
Hammer-ons
Slide
Also read Appendices Two and Four

In Lesson Twenty Eight riffs 1-15 were analysed with regard to the scale upon which they were based. The following table analyses riffs 16-28.

RIFF	BLUES	MAJOR	MINOR
16	✗		
17			✗ Harmonic
18	✗		
19		✗ + Passing Notes	
20			✗ "Pure" + Passing Notes
21	✗ + Passing Notes		
22	✗		
23	✗		
24	✗ + Passing Notes		
25	✗ + Passing Notes		
26		✗ + Passing Notes	
27			✗ "Pure"
28		✗	

SECTION THREE

Section III introduces the student to the concept of creating his/her own bass lines. Arpeggios of the most common chords are introduced, together with the theory of chord construction.

PAUL McCARTNEY

LESSON THIRTY NINE

CREATING A BASS LINE

There are several approaches which can be used to create a bass line for a given chord progression (or song). These are listed below:

1. Root note bass.
2. Riff playing (based on scales).
3. Walking bass (based on scales and passing notes).
4. Chord notes (based on chord construction).

Examples of the first 3 approaches have been used in Sections One and Two, and discussed in detail. Approach 4, using chord notes, is based upon chord construction.

CHORD CONSTRUCTION – MAJOR CHORDS

Every chord type (i.e. major, minor, 7th etc.) is based upon a specific formula which relates back to the major scale after which it is named (revise major scales, outlined in Appendix Two). The formula for a major chord is $\overline{\text{I}}$-$\overline{\text{III}}$-$\overline{\text{V}}$, hence the C major chord consists of the first, third and fifth notes of the C major scale.

C major scale:

C	D	E	F	G	A	B	C
I	II	III	IV	V	VI	VII	VIII

C major chord:

C	E	G
I	III	V

Now consider the D major chord, which is constructed from the D major scale:

D major scale:

D	E	F#	G	A	B	C#	D
I	II	III	IV	V	VI	VII	VIII

D major chord:

D	F#	A
I	III	V

or the E♭ major chord:

E♭ major scale:

E♭	F	G	A♭	B♭	C	D	E♭
I	II	III	IV	V	VI	VII	VIII

E♭ major chord: E♭ G B♭

It is important for you to revise all major scales so far studied. Once you have done this, construct the following chords.

G F A E B♭

MAJOR CHORD ARPEGGIO

In the following progression, a riff is created by using chord notes.

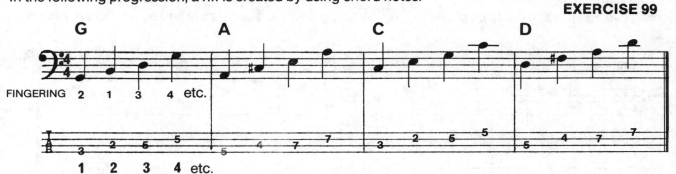

The chord notes in the above progression are played in the order Ī-ĪĪĪ-V̄-V̄ĪĪĪ. This is an example of **arpeggio** playing (i.e. playing a chord in note form). It creates the following pattern on the fretboard.

Major chord arpeggio
Commencing on the 4th string

Major chord arpeggio
Commencing on the 3rd string

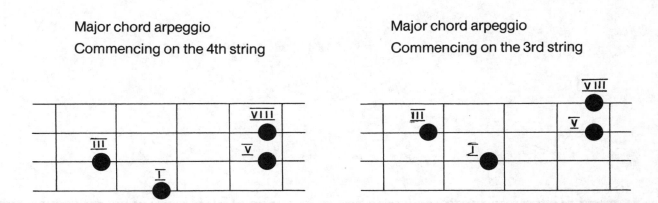

Play the following major chord arpeggio exercises.

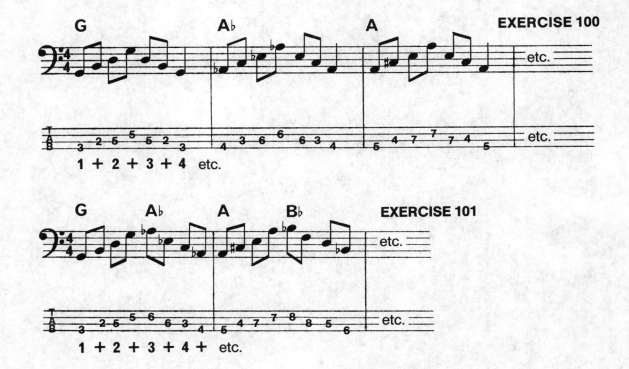

In arpeggio playing it is possible to use any combination of the chord notes and also any timing variations. For example, Exercise 98 could be played $\overline{\text{I}}$-$\overline{\text{III}}$-$\overline{\text{VIII}}$-$\overline{\text{V}}$ using a dotted quarter note and eighth note rhythm as such:

EXERCISE 102

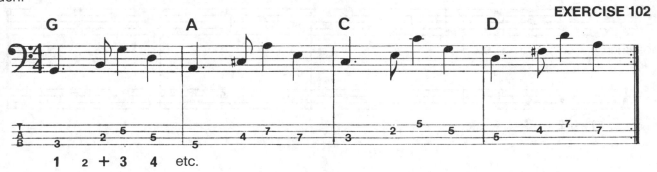

Experiment with other arpeggio and timing combinations. Lesson Forty Seven summarizes and expands upon the arpeggios studied in this section.

AC/DC (Courtesy EMI)

LESSON FORTY

MINOR CHORD CONSTRUCTION

In the previous lesson you were introduced to the major chord formula, $\underline{I}$-$\underline{III}$-$\underline{V}$. The formula for a minor chord is $\underline{I}$-$\underline{III}\flat$-$\underline{V}$, thus the only difference between a major and a minor chord is the flattened third note.

e.g. Notes of the C major scale:

C	D	E	F	G	A	B	C
$\underline{I}$	$\underline{II}$	$\underline{III}$	$\underline{IV}$	$\underline{V}$	$\underline{VI}$	$\underline{VII}$	$\underline{VIII}$

Notes of the C minor chord:

C		E♭		G
$\underline{I}$		$\underline{III}\flat$		$\underline{V}$

You will notice that although the chord type is minor, its notes are derived from the major scale, not the minor scale.

Comparing the C major and C minor chord notes, only the $\underline{III}$ is different (i.e. E in C major as compared to E♭ in C minor).

C: C E G   Cm: C E♭ G
$\underline{I}$ $\underline{III}$ $\underline{V}$ $\underline{I}$ $\underline{III}\flat$ $\underline{V}$

Now, looking at the E major scale:

E	F#	G#	A	B	C#	D#	E
$\underline{I}$	$\underline{II}$	$\underline{III}$	$\underline{IV}$	$\underline{V}$	$\underline{VI}$	$\underline{VII}$	$\underline{VIII}$

The E major and E minor chords contain the notes:

E: E G# B   Em: E G B
$\underline{I}$ $\underline{III}$ $\underline{V}$ $\underline{I}$ $\underline{III}\flat$ $\underline{V}$

Construct the following minor chords:

Am   Dm   Gm   Fm

MINOR CHORD ARPEGGIO

The minor chord arpeggio forms the following patterns on the fretboard.

Minor chord arpeggio
Commencing on the 4th string

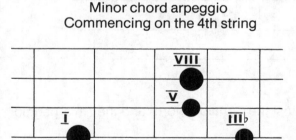

Minor chord arpeggio
Commencing on the 3rd string

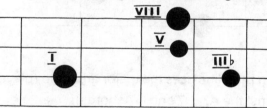

Play the following arpeggio exercise.

8 BAR MINOR BLUES

EXERCISE 103

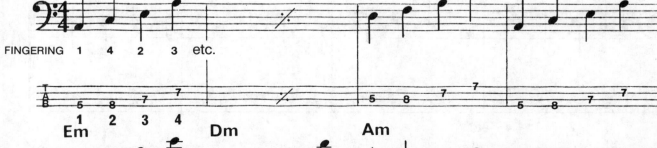

FINGERING   1   4   2   3   etc.

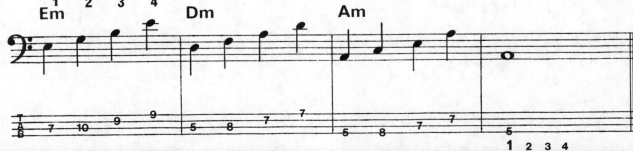

LESSON FORTY ONE

7TH CHORD CONSTRUCTION

The 7th chord (correctly called "dominant 7th") is formed by adding a flattened 7th note to the major chord:

$$\underline{I} \quad \underline{III} \quad \underline{V} \quad \underline{VII}\flat$$

The C7 chord is constructed from the C major scale as such:

C major scale:	C	D	E	F	G	A	B	C
	$\underline{I}$	$\underline{II}$	$\underline{III}$	$\underline{IV}$	$\underline{V}$	$\underline{VI}$	$\underline{VII}$	$\underline{VIII}$
C7:	C		E		G		B♭	
	$\underline{I}$		$\underline{III}$		$\underline{V}$		$\underline{VII}\flat$	

The A7 chord is constructed from the A major scale:

A major scale:	A	B	C#	D	E	F#	G#	A
	$\underline{I}$	$\underline{II}$	$\underline{III}$	$\underline{IV}$	$\underline{V}$	$\underline{VI}$	$\underline{VII}$	$\underline{VIII}$
A7:	A		C#		E		G	
	$\underline{I}$		$\underline{III}$		$\underline{V}$		$\underline{VII}\flat$	

Remember to check the sharps or flats involved in each scale when working out the notes of a chord.

Construct the following 7th chords:

D7   G7   E7   B♭7

7TH CHORD ARPEGGIO

The 7th chord arpeggio forms the following pattern on the fretboard:

7th chord arpeggio
Commencing on the 4th string

7th chord arpeggio
Commencing on the 3rd string

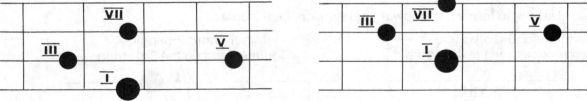

The following bass line uses the major arpeggio (played against the C major chord) and the 7th arpeggio (played against the A7, D7 and G7 chords).

EXERCISE 104

LESSON FORTY TWO

THE $\overline{I}$-$\overline{V}$ FORMULA

The three chord formulas you have so far studied; major, minor and 7th, are summarized below using C as an example.

C major	C	E	G	
	$\overline{I}$	$\overline{III}$	$\overline{V}$	
C minor	C	E♭	G	
	$\overline{I}$	$\overline{III}$♭	$\overline{V}$	
C7	C	E	G	B♭
	$\overline{I}$	$\overline{III}$	$\overline{V}$	$\overline{VII}$♭

From this table, you will notice that the C and G notes ($\overline{I}$ and $\overline{V}$) are common to all three chord types. A simple approach for creating a bass line is to use only these notes, referred to as the "$\overline{I}$-$\overline{V}$ formula". Previous examples of the $\overline{I}$-$\overline{V}$ formula occurred in the following exercises:

Ex. 11 — 12 Bar in C ($\overline{I}$-$\overline{V}$)

Ex. 46 — Turnaround one in A ($\overline{I}$-$\overline{V}$-$\overline{I}$)

Ex. 48 — Turnaround two in A ($\overline{I}$-$\overline{V}$-$\overline{VIII}$*)

Ex. 76 — Reggae ($\overline{I}$-$\overline{V}$)

Ex. 78 — Bossa Nova (2 bar: $\overline{I}$-$\overline{V}$-$\overline{VIII}$-$\overline{V}$-$\overline{I}$)

Ex. 79 — Samba ($\overline{I}$-$\overline{V}$-$\overline{VIII}$)

The $\overline{I}$-$\overline{V}$ formula produces the following patterns on the fretboard:

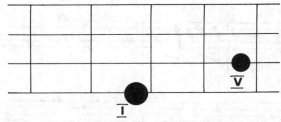

This pattern can commence on either the 4th, 3rd or 2nd strings and was used in exercises 46 and 76.

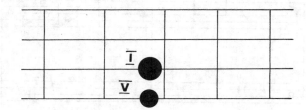

This pattern can commence on either the 3rd, 2nd or 1st string and was used in exercise 11.

---

* $\overline{VIII}$ is the $\overline{I}$ note an octave higher.

Adding the VIII gives the following patterns:

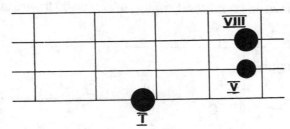

This pattern can commence on either the 4th or 3rd strings.

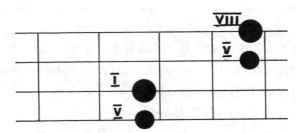

This pattern can only commence on the 3rd string.

The following bass line uses the I-V formula and also introduces the key signature of A major (see "Key Signatures" in Appendix Two. Be sure to sharpen all F, C and G notes as indicated by this signature.

EXERCISE 105

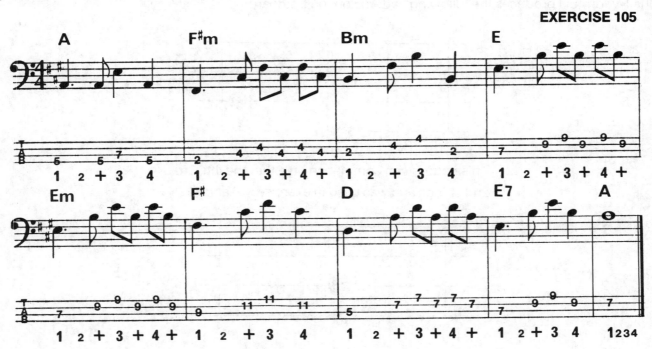

Use the above progression to create your own bass lines.

LESSON FORTY THREE

MAJOR 7TH*, MINOR 7TH AND NINTH CHORD CONSTRUCTION

The formula for the major 7th chord is:

$$\underline{\text{I}} \quad \underline{\text{III}} \quad \underline{\text{V}} \quad \underline{\text{VII}}$$

So a Cmaj7 chord contains the notes C-E-G-B, and an Amaj7 chord contains the notes A-C#-E-G#.

The major 7th chord arpeggio forms the following patterns on the fretboard:

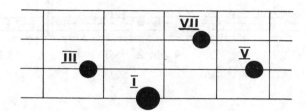

This pattern can commence on either the 4th or 3rd strings.

The formula for the minor 7th chord is:

$$\underline{\text{I}} \quad \underline{\text{III}}\flat \quad \underline{\text{V}} \quad \underline{\text{VII}}\flat$$

So a Cm 7 chord contains the notes C-E♭-G-B♭, and an Am 7 chord contains the notes A-C-E-G.

The minor 7th chord arpeggio forms the following pattern on the fretboard:

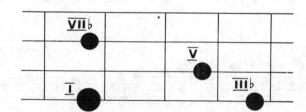

This pattern can commence on either the 4th or 3rd strings.

The formula for the ninth chord is:

$$\underline{\text{I}} \quad \underline{\text{III}} \quad \underline{\text{V}} \quad \underline{\text{VII}}\flat \quad \underline{\text{IX}}$$

So a C9 chord contains the notes C-E-G-B♭*-D, and an A9 chord contains the notes A-C#-E-G-B.

The ninth chord arpeggio forms the following pattern on the fretboard:

This pattern can only commence on the 4th string.

* Do not confuse major 7th chords with 7th chords (dominant 7th).

84

The following chord progression, using major 7th, minor 7th and ninth chords is a "jazz" variation of the turnaround.

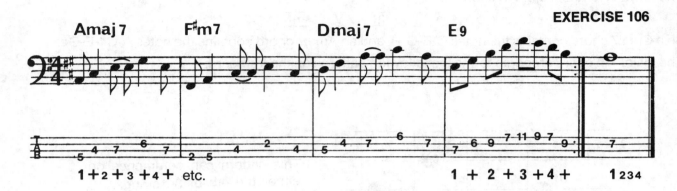

As a variation to the above bass line, scale notes can be added.

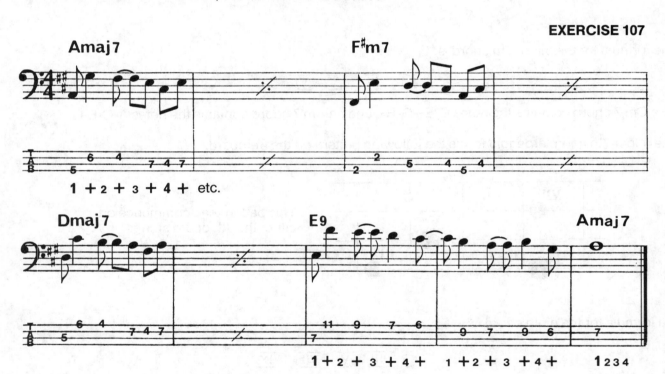

LESSON FORTY FOUR

SUSPENDED CHORD CONSTRUCTION

In sheet music, the suspended chord is often written as "sus" e.g. A sus indicating A suspended. It can also be written as "sus4".

The formula for a suspended chord is $\overline{I}$-$\overline{IV}$-$\overline{V}$, so a Csus chord contains the notes C-F-G, and an Asus chord contains the notes A-D-E.

The suspended chord arpeggio forms the following pattern on the fretboard:

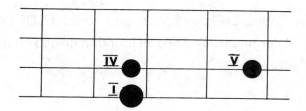

This pattern can commence on either the 4th or 3rd strings.

The following bass line combines the suspended chord arpeggio with the major chord arpeggio, and is played in $\frac{3}{4}$ time.

EXERCISE 108

LESSON FORTY FIVE

DIMINISHED CHORD CONSTRUCTION

The formula for a diminished chord (often abbreviated to "dim." or written with a small ° or a minus sign) is:

$$\underline{\text{I}} \qquad \underline{\text{III}}\flat \qquad \underline{\text{V}}\flat \qquad \underline{\text{VII}}\flat\flat \, *$$

Thus the G° chord is constructed as such:

G   B♭   D♭   F♭ (E)

and the B♭° chord is constructed:

B♭   D♭   F♭ (E)   A♭♭ (G)

You will notice that the notes contained in these two chords are identical. If you construct a D° or an E° they will also contain the same notes (arranged in a different order). Thus all four diminished chords will use the following arpeggio pattern:

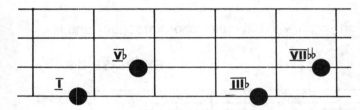

This pattern can commence on either the 4th, 3rd or 2nd strings. Each note of the pattern can be regarded as a root note of the four respective diminished chords.

Play the following diminished chord exercises.

* A double flat sign (♭♭) lowers the note's pitch by one tone (2 semi-tones).

LESSON FORTY SIX

AUGMENTED CHORD CONSTRUCTION

The formula for an augmented chord (abbreviated to "aug", or +) is:

$$\underline{I} \quad \underline{III} \quad \underline{V}\#$$

	$\underline{I}$	$\underline{III}$	$\underline{V}\#$
Thus the C+ is constructed:	C	E	G#
and the E+ is constructed:	E	G#	B# (C)

As with diminished chords, the above two examples use identical notes, and a G#+ will also contain the same notes. They will all use the following arpeggio pattern:

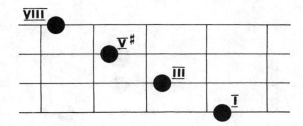

SIXTH CHORD CONSTRUCTION

The 6th chord contains the $\underline{I}$-$\underline{III}$-$\underline{V}$-$\underline{VI}$ notes of the major scale. Thus a G6 contains the notes G-B-D-E and a C6 contains the notes C-E-G—A. The sixth chord forms the following arpeggio pattern on the fretboard:

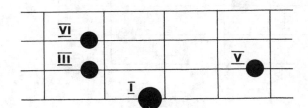

This pattern can commence on either the 4th or 3rd strings.

The following bass line uses the augmented and sixth chord arpeggios studied in this lesson.

EXERCISE 111

LESSON FORTY SEVEN

ARPEGGIO PATTERNS

This lesson summarises all of the arpeggio patterns studied in Section $\overline{III}$. Other useful patterns have also been included.

Practice each of these arpeggios as outlined in exercises 100 and 101.

MAJOR

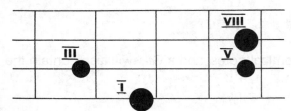
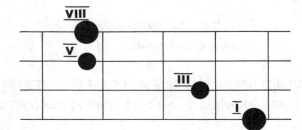

MINOR

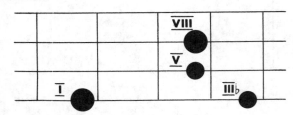
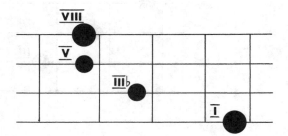

SEVENTH

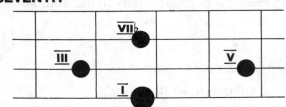
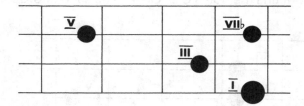

MAJOR SEVENTH

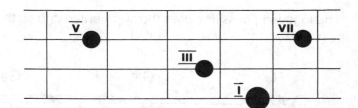

MINOR SEVENTH

NINTH

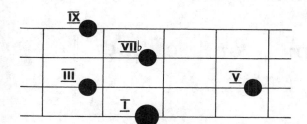

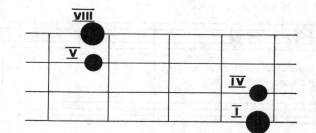

SUSPENDED

DIMINISHED

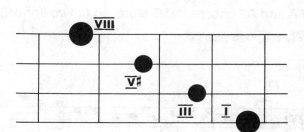

AUGMENTED

SIXTH

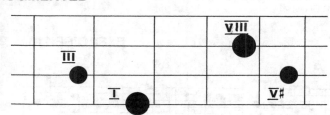

LESSON FORTY EIGHT

COMPARISON OF STYLES

The following chord progression has been used to illustrate the four approaches to creating a bass line:

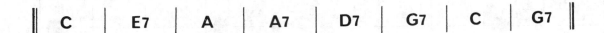

ROOT NOTE BASS:

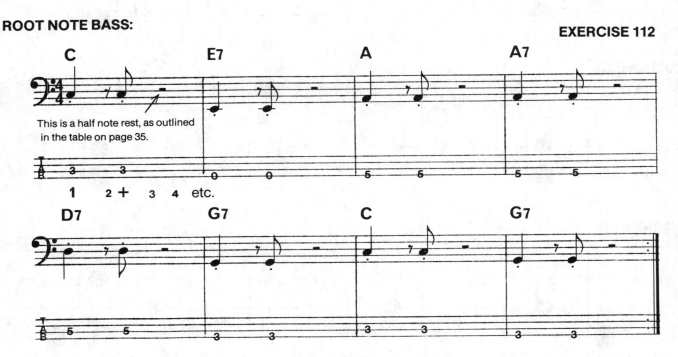

RIFF STYLE: The following exercise combines three different riffs. For the C major chord, riff 2 is played; for the A and A7 chords, riff 5 is played (a two bar riff) and for the 7th chords a new riff based on the 7th chord arpeggio is played.

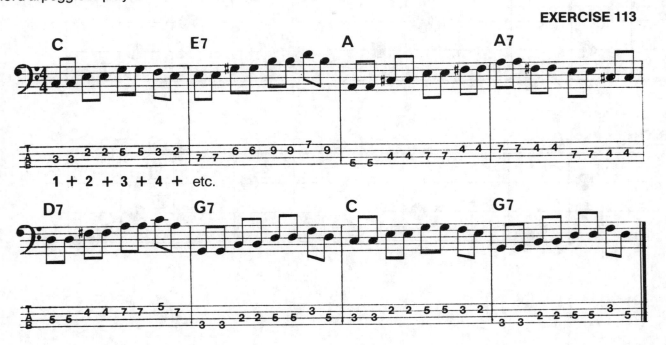

WALKING BASS:

ARPEGGIO STYLE:

Your choice of approach will depend on the "feel" of the song, which incorporates aspects such as melody, rhythm and tempo. For example, the riff style of playing is more suited to a song with a rock feel, whereas the walking bass may be more suited to a song with a jazz feel.

APPENDIX ONE –
TUNING

It is essential for your bass to be in tune, so that the notes you play will sound correct. The main problem with tuning for most beginning students is that the ear is not able to determine slight differences in pitch. For this reason you should seek the aid of a teacher or an experienced bass player.

Several methods can be used to tune the bass. These include:

1.   Tuning to another musical instrument (e.g. a piano, or another guitar).
2.   Tuning to pitch pipes or a tuning fork.
3.   Tuning the bass to itself.

The most common and useful of these is the latter; tuning the bass to itself. This method involves finding notes of the same pitch on different strings. The diagram below outlines the notes used:

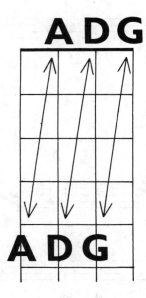

The method of tuning is as follows:

1.   Tune the open 4th string to either:
    (a)   The open 4th string of another bass.
    (b)   Tune to a guitar.
    (c)   A Piano.

On the guitar, the lowest strings correspond to the 4 strings of the bass. (i.e. EADG), but are an octave higher.

On the piano, the note equivalent to the open 4th string is indicated on the diagram below.

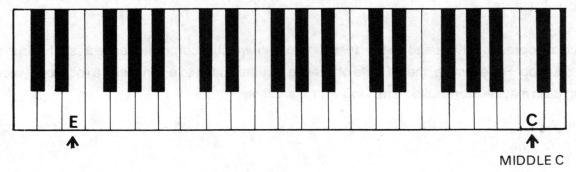

MIDDLE C

(d) Pitch pipes, which produce notes that correspond with each of the 4 open strings.

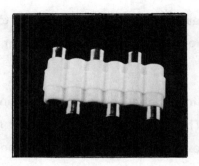

2. Place a finger on the 4th string at the 5th fret. Now play the open A 3rd string. if the guitar is to be in tune, then these two notes must have the same pitch (i.e. sound the same). If they do not sound the same, the 3rd string must be adjusted to match the note produced on the 4th string, i.e. it is tuned in relation to the 4th string.

3. Tune the open 2nd string to the note on the 5th fret of the 3rd string, using the method outlined above.

4. Tune the open 1st string to the note on the 5th fret of the second string.

TUNING HINTS

One of the easiest ways to practice tuning is to actually start with the bass in tune and then de-tune one string. When you do this, always take the string down in pitch (i.e. loosen it) as it is easier to tune 'up' to a given note rather than 'down' to it. As an example, de-tune the 2nd string (D). If you play a riff or scale now, the bass will sound out of tune, even though only one string has been altered (so remember that if your bass is out of tune it may only be one string at fault).

Following the correct method, you must tune the 2nd string against the D note at the 5th fret of the 3rd string. Play the note loudly, and listen carefully to the sound produced. This will help you retain the correct pitch in your mind when tuning the next string.

Now that you have listened carefully to the note that you want, the D string must be tuned to it. Pluck the D string, and turn its tuning key at the same time, and you will hear the pitch of the string change (it will become higher as the tuning key tightens the string). It is important to follow this procedure, so that you hear the sound of the string at all times, as it tightens. You should also constantly refer back to the correct sound that is required (i.e. the D note on the 5th fret of the 3rd string).

APPENDIX TWO – MUSIC THEORY

MUSIC THEORY

This appendix will cover some essential areas of music theory that relate to the material studied in this book. All of the theory in this section should be thoroughly understood and learnt.

THE MAJOR SCALE

A scale can be defined as a series of notes in alphabetical order, progressing from any one note to its octave, and based upon a given set pattern. The pattern upon which the major scale is based is that of tone—tone—semitone—tone—tone—tone—semitone, eg. Starting on the C note and following through this pattern gives the C major scale:

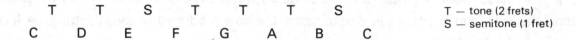

T	T	S	T	T	T	S		T — tone (2 frets)
C	D	E	F	G	A	B	C	S — semitone (1 fret)

and in musical notation:

Treble Clef – used by vocalists, guitarists, pianists, etc.

MIDDLE C

Bass Clef – used by bass guitarists, pianists, etc.

C D E F G A B C

The major scale will always give the familiar sound of DO, RA, ME, FA, SO, LA, TE, DO.

It is important to remember that the major scale always uses the same pattern of tones and semitones, no matter what note is used as the tonic (starting note). Here are seven more major scales:

	T	T	S	T	T	T	S	
G major:	G	A	B	C	D	E	F#	G
D major:	D	E	F#	G	A	B	C#	D
A major:	A	B	C#	D	E	F#	G#	A
E major:	E	F#	G#	A	B	C#	D#	E
F major:	F	G	A	Bb	C	D	E	F
Bb major:	Bb	C	D	Eb	F	G	A	Bb
Eb major:	Eb	F	G	Ab	Bb	C	D	Eb

KEY SIGNATURES

When music is talked of as being in a particular key, it means that the melody is based upon notes of the major scale with the same name, e.g. in the key of C, C major scale notes (i.e. C, D, E, F, G, A and B) will occur much more frequently than notes that do not belong to the C scale (i.e. sharpened and flattened notes). This same principle applies to a bass line.

In the key of G, G scale notes will be most common (i.e. the notes G, A, B, C, D, E and F# will occur frequently). You will notice here that F# occurs rather than F natural. However, rather than add a sharp to every F note, an easier method is used whereby a sharp sign is placed on the F line (the second line from the top) of the staff at the beginning of each line. This is referred to as the key signature: thus the key signature of G major is F#.

Written below are the key signatures for all eight scales so far discussed.

It can be seen, then, that each key signature is a shorthand representation of the scale, showing only the sharps or flats which occur in that scale. Where an additional sharp or flat occurs, it is not included as part of the key signature, but is written in the music, eg. in the key of G, if a D# note occurs, the sharp sign will be written immediately before the D note, **not** at the beginning of the line as part of the key signature.

MINOR KEYS AND SCALES

Our discussion of major scales revealed that each key is based on a scale of the same name and that the key features the scale notes predominantly, eg. the key of F major features the notes F, G, A, B♭, C, D and E.

Many songs, however, are written in a minor key, which involves the use of minor scales. For each minor key, three minor scales exist. These three minor scales are written below, using the key of A minor as an example:

KEY OF A MINOR

A minor "pure" scale
(Aeolian mode):

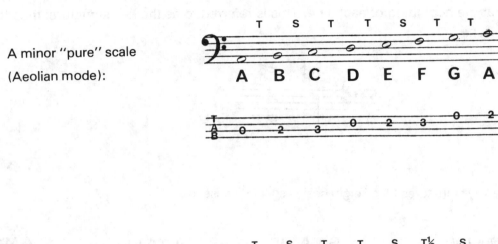

A minor Harmonic —
7th note sharpened.

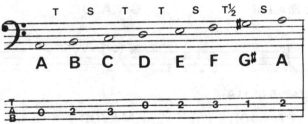

A minor Melodic — 6th and 7th notes sharpened when ascending and returned to natural when descending.

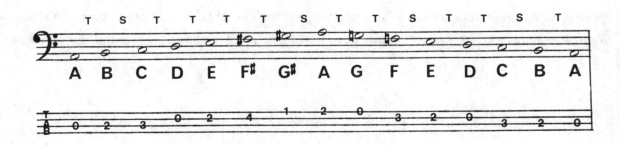

If you compare the A minor "pure" scale with the C major scale you will notice that they contain the same notes (except starting on a different note). Because of this, these two scales are referred to as being "relatives"; A minor is the relative minor of C major and vice versa.

For every major scale there is a relative minor, as listed in the table below. On the bass guitar the root note of the relative minor is located three frets lower than its relative major. e.g. C major root 6 bar chord – 8th fret; A minor root 6 bar chord – 5th fret.

MAJOR KEY	C	D♭	D	E♭	E	F	F♯	G	A♭	A	B♭	B
RELATIVE MINOR KEY:	Am	B♭m	Bm	Cm	C♯m	Dm	D♯m	Em	Fm	F♯m	Gm	G♯m

The major key and its relative minor both share the same key signature, eg. a key signature of F sharp could indicate either the key of G major, or the key of E minor. To determine the correct key, you can:

a.   Look for the 7th note of the minor scale. This is the only note of a minor scale (except the "pure" minor) which is not found in its relative major, eg. a D♯ note in the melody will strongly suggest the key of E minor, rather than G major.

b.   Look at the finishing note of the piece, because a song very often finishes on its root note, eg. a song finishing on a G note would suggest the key of G major (Quite often the beginning and ending chords will also indicate the key in the same manner).

These are guidelines only and should not be taken as strict rules.

SCALE TONE CHORD ARPEGGIOS

In any given key certain chords are more common than others. For example, in the key of C the chords, C, F and G are usually present, and quite often the chords Am, Dm and Em occur. The reason for this is that each key has its own set of chords, which are constructed from notes of its major scale. These chords are referred to as 'scale tone' chords.

Consider the C major scale:

C	D	E	F	G	A	B	C
I	II	III	IV	V	VI	VII	VIII

Chords are constructed by combining notes which are a third apart. For example, consider the formula for a major chord:

Using the C major scale written above, scale tone chords can be constructed by placing 2 third intervals above each note. This is illustrated in the table below:

$\underline{V}$	G	A	B	C	D	E	F	G
$\underline{III}$	E	F	G	A	B	C	D	E
C Scale:	C	D	E	F	G	A	B	C
Chord Constructed:	C	Dm	Em	F	G	Am	B⁰	C

) Third Interval
) Third Interval

Notice that the chords are named according to their root note (and hence use the root note's scale). However, they are all C scale tone chords because they contain only notes of the C scale (i.e. no sharps or flats).

The method used for constructing scale tone chords in the key of C may be applied to any major scale. The result will always produce the following scale tone chords:

Scale note:	$\underline{I}$	$\underline{II}$	$\underline{III}$	$\underline{IV}$	$\underline{V}$	$\underline{VI}$	$\underline{VII}$	$\underline{VIII}$
Chord Constructed:	major	minor	minor	major	major	minor	diminished	major

Thus in the key of G major, the scale tone chords will be:

G   Am   Bm   C   D   Em   F#⁰   G

and the key of E♭ major, the scale tone chords will be:

E♭   Fm   Gm   A♭   B♭   Cm   D⁰   E♭

SCALE TONE CHORD EXTENSIONS

The scale tone chords studied so far involve the placement of two notes (separated by an interval of a third) above a root note. This method of building scale tone chords can be extended by adding another note, illustrated in the following table:

$\underline{VII}$	B	C	D	E	F	G	A	B
$\underline{V}$	G	A	B	C	D	E	F	G
$\underline{III}$	E	F	G	A	B	C	D	E
C Scale:	C	D	E	F	G	A	B	C
Chord constructed:	Cmaj7	Dm7	Em7	Fmaj7	G7	Am7	Bø7*	Cmaj7

) Third Interval
) Third Interval
) Third Interval

From this example, the scale tone chords for any key will be:

$\underline{I}$	$\underline{II}$	$\underline{III}$	$\underline{IV}$	$\underline{V}$	$\underline{VI}$	$\underline{VII}$	$\underline{VIII}$
major 7	m7	m7	maj7	dom7	m7	ø7	maj7

ALTERED CHORDS

Other chords that you will occasionally see in sheet music involve a slight alteration to one of the given formulas. The alteration is usually indicated in the name given to the chord. Consider the following examples:

C7:   C   E   G   B♭   C7♭5:   C   E   G♭   B♭

The C7♭5 chord is just as the name implies; a C7 chord with the fifth note flattened. Thus the C7♭5 arpeggio will be:

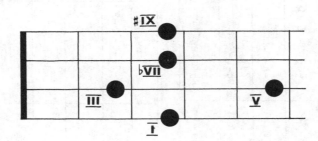

G9:   G   B   D   F   A
G7♯9:   G   B   D   F   A♯

The G7#9 chord involves sharpening the 9th note of the G9 chord.

G7#9 Arpeggio:

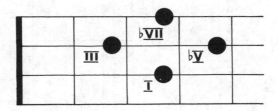

Another type of alteration occurs when chord symbole are written as G/F# bass. This indicates that an F# bass note is played against the G chord. Sometimes the word 'bass' will not be written (i.e. the symbol will be just G/F#), but the same meaning is implied.

CHORD FORMULA CHART

The following chart lists chord formulas for the 8 most common keys. Other chords not listed can be derived by applying the correct formula to the respective scale, e.g.

B7 is based on the dom7 formula ($\overline{I}$-$\overline{III}$-$\overline{V}$-$\overline{VII}$♭), and the B scale:

| | B | C♯ | D♯ | E | F♯ | G♯ | A♯ | B |

Thus:

| | $\overline{I}$ | | $\overline{III}$ | | $\overline{V}$ | | $\overline{VII}$♭ | |
| | B | | D♯ | | F♯ | | A | |

CHORD FORMULA CHART

KEY	MAJOR	MAJ 6	MAJ 7	MAJ 9	DOM 7	DOM 9	11	13
	1-3-5	1-3-5-6	1-3-5-7	1-3-5-7-9	1-3-5-7b	1-3-5-7b-9	1-3-5-7b-9-11	1-3-5-7b-9-13
C MAJOR No Sharps or Flats	C-E-G	C-E-G-A	C-E-G-B	C-E-G-B-D	C-E-G-Bb	C-E-G-Bb-D	C-E-G-Bb-D-F	C-E-G-Bb-D-A
G MAJOR F#	G-B-D	G-B-D-E	G-B-D-F#	G-B-D-F#-A	G-B-D-F	G-B-D-F-A	G-B-D-F-A-C	G-B-D-F-A-E
D MAJOR F#, C#	D-F#-A	D-F#-A-B	D-F#-A-C#	D-F#-A-C#-E	D-F#-A-C	D-F#-A-C-E	D-F#-A-C-E-G	D-F#-A-C-E-B
A MAJOR F#, C#, G#	A-C#-E	A-C#-E-F#	A-C#-E-G#	A-C#-E-G#-B	A-C#-E-G	A-C#-E-G-B	A-C#-E-G-B-D	A-C#-E-G-B-F#
E MAJOR F#, C#, G#, D#	E-G#-B	E-G#-B-C#	E-G#-B-D#	E-G#-B-D#-F#	E-G#-B-D	E-G#-B-D-F#	E-G#-B-D-F#-A	E-G#-B-D-F#-C#
F MAJOR Bb	F-A-C	F-A-C-D	F-A-C-E	F-A-C-E-G	F-A-C-Eb	F-A-C-Eb-G	F-A-C-Eb-G-Bb	F-A-C-Eb-G-D
Bb MAJOR Bb, Eb	Bb-D-F	Bb-D-F-G	Bb-D-F-A	Bb-D-F-A-C	Bb-D-F-Ab	Bb-D-F-Ab-C	Bb-D-F-Ab-C-Eb	Bb-D-F-Ab-C-G
Eb MAJOR Bb, Eb, Ab	Eb-G-Bb	Eb-G-Bb-C	Eb-G-Bb-D	Eb-G-Bb-D-F	Eb-G-Bb-Db	Eb-G-Bb-Db-F	Eb-G-Bb-Db-F-Ab	Eb-G-Bb-Db-F-C

KEY	MINOR	m6	m7	m9	AUG	HALF DIMINISHED (ø)	DIMINISHED (o)	SUSPENDED
	1-3b-5	1-3b-5-6	1-3b-5-7b	1-3b-5-7b-9	1-3-5#	1-3b-5b-7b	1-3b-5b-7bb	1-4-5
C MAJOR No Sharps or Flats	C-Eb-G	C-Eb-G-A	C-Eb-G-Bb	C-Eb-G-Bb-D	C-E-G#	C-Eb-Gb-Bb	C-Eb-Gb-Bbb	C-F-G
G MAJOR F#	G-Bb-D	G-Bb-D-E	G-Bb-D-F	G-Bb-D-F-A	G-B-D#	G-Bb-Db-F	G-Bb-Db-Fb	G-C-D
D MAJOR F#, C#	D-F-A	D-F-A-B	D-F-A-C	D-F-A-C-E	D-F#-A#	D-F-Ab-C	D-F-Ab-Cb	D-G-A
A MAJOR F#, C#, G#	A-C-E	A-C-E-F#	A-C-E-G	A-C-E-G-B	A-C#-E#	A-C-Eb-G	A-C-Eb-Gb	A-D-E
E MAJOR F#, C#, G#, D#	E-G-B	E-G-B-C#	E-G-B-D	E-G-B-D-F#	E-G#-B#	E-G-Bb-D	E-G-Bb-Db	E-A-B
F MAJOR Bb	F-Ab-C	F-Ab-C-D	F-Ab-C-Eb	F-Ab-C-Eb-G	F-A-C#	F-Ab-Cb-Eb	F-Ab-Cb-Ebb	F-Bb-C
Bb MAJOR Bb, Eb	Bb-Db-F	Bb-Db-F-G	Bb-Db-F-Ab	Bb-Db-F-Ab-C	Bb-D-F#	Bb-Db-Fb-Ab	Bb-Db-Fb-Abb	Bb-Eb-F
Eb MAJOR Bb, Eb, Ab	Eb-Gb-Bb	Eb-Gb-Bb-C	Eb-Gb-Bb-Db	Eb-Gb-Bb-Db-F	Eb-G-B	Eb-Gb-Bbb-Db	Eb-Gb-Bbb-Dbb	Eb-Ab-Bb

APPENDIX THREE – SONG LIST

In modern music there are several standard chord progressions that are the basis of many songs. The most common of these progressions are "Turnarounds" and "Twelve Bar Blues".

TURNAROUNDS

There are two main turnarounds, which are labelled Turnaround One and Turnaround Two.

TURNAROUND ONE: Key of C:

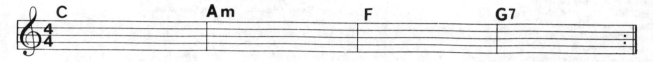

This turnaround can be transposed to any key. Here is the same turnaround in the key of G, playing two chords per bar.

Written below is a list of songs which use turnaround one.

The night has a 1,000 Eyes — Bobby Vee
It's Raining Again — Supertramp
More — Various artists
Ti Amo — Umberto Tozzi
Crocodile Rock (chorus) — Elton John
One Last Kiss — Various Artists
Stand by Me — John Lennon
Dream — Everly Brothers
Return to Sender — Elvis Presley
Telstar — Tornadoes
Always Look on the Bright side of Life — Monty Python
Why do fools fall in love — Frankie Lyman/Diana Ross
Sarah — Fleetwood Mac
Take Good Care of my Baby — Bobby Vee/Smokie
Where have all the Flowers Gone — Various Artists
Runaround Sue — Dion & the Belmonts
Tell me Why — Beatles
Let's Twist Again — Chubby Checker
Stay (Just a Little Bit Longer) — Four Seasons/Jackson Brown
Cool for Cats — U.K. Squeeze
Y.M.C.A. — Village People
Tired of toein' the Line — Rocky Burnett
You Drive Me Crazy — Shakin' Stevens
Should I do it — Pointer Sisters
Poor Little Fool — Rick Nelson
You Don't have to say you Love Me — Dusty Springfield/Elvis Presley
Breaking up is hard to do — Neil Sedaka/Partridge Family
Oh Carol — Neil Sedaka
Two Faces Have I — Lou Christie
Every Day — Buddy Holly
Poetry in Motion — Johnny Tillotson
Sweet Little 16 — Neil Sedaka
Big Girls Don't Cry — Four Seasons
Sherry — Four Seasons
How Do you do it — Jerry & the Pacemakers
Shout, Shout — Rocky Sharp and The Replays
Aces With You — Moon Martin
If I Had a Hammer — Peter, Paul & Mary
Every Breath You Take — Police
Telephone — Sheena Easton
Rain Until September — Carol King
Fraction Too Much Friction — Tim Finn

Joane — Michael Nesmith
Goodnight Sweetheart — Various artists
Looking for an Echo — Ol' 55
Summer Holiday — Cliff Richard
Be My Baby — The Ronettes/Rachel Sweet
Everlasting Love — Rachel Sweet/Love Affair
I Go To Pieces (verse) — Peter & Gordon
Love Hurts — Everly Brothers/Jim Capaldi/Nazareth
Gee Baby — Peter Shelley
Classic — Adrian Gurvitz
Teenage Dream — T-Rex
Blue Moon -- Various Artists
The Tide is High — Blondie
Dennis — Blondie
It Ain't Easy — Normie Rowe
My World — Bee Gees
Hey Paula — Various Artists
It's Only Make Believe — Glen Campbell
Can't Smile Without You — Barry Manilow
Take Good Care of my Baby — Bobby Vee/Smokie
Crossfire — Bellamy Brothers
Bobby's Girl — Marcie Blane
Do that to me one more time — Captain and Tenille
Please Mr. Postman — Carpenters/Beatles
Sharin' the Night Together — Dr. Hook
9 to 5 (Morning Train) — Sheena Easton
Diana — Paul Anka
Telstar — Tornadoes
Enola Gay — Orchestral Manoeuvres in the Dark
Some Guys have all the Luck — Robert Palmer
So Lonely — Get Wet
Hungry Heart — Bruce Springsteen
Land of Make Believe (chorus) — Bucks Fizz
Daddys Home — Cliff Richard
The Wonder of You — Elvis Presley
So You Win Again — Hot Chocolate
Hang Five — Rolling Stones
Paper Tiger — Sue Thompson
Rain — Dragon
My Boyfriend's Back — Melissa Manchester
Words — F. R. David

* Some of the songs listed under 'Turnarounds' vary from the basic structure of this progression. For example, the turnaround progression may be used in the verses, but not in the chorus.

TURNAROUND TWO:

Turnaround two uses a different minor chord in the second bar.

Key of C:

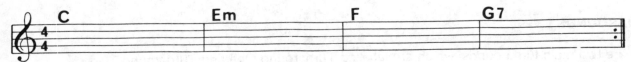

Written below is a list of songs which use turnaround two.

Crocodile Rock (verse) — Elton John
I Started a Joke — Bee Gees
Different Drum — Linda Rhonstadt
Key Largo — Bertie Higgins
Black Berry Way — The Move
Georgy Girl — Seekers
Where Do You Go to My Lovely — Peter Sarsted
Mrs. Brown, You've Got a Lovely Daughter — Hermans Hermit
Toast and Marmalade for Tea — Tin Tin
Movie Star — Harpo
Where did our Love Go — Diana Ross & The Supremes

I Go To Pieces (chorus) — Peter & Gordon
Get it over with — Angie Gold
Sad Sweet Dreamer — Sweet Sensation
Down Town — Petula Clark
Easy — Oakridge Boys
It's a Heartache — Bonnie Tyler
I Don't Like Mondays — Boomtown Rats
My Angel Baby — Toby Beau
Land of Make Believe (verse) — Bucks Fizz
I'm in the mood for Dancing — The Nolans
What's in a Kiss — Gilbert O'Sullivan
My Baby Loves Love — Joe Jefferies
Dreamin' — Jonny Burnett
Cruel to be Kind — Nick Lowe

12 BAR BLUES

12 Bar Blues is a set pattern of chords which repeats every 12 bars. Here is a 12 Bar Blues in the key of A:

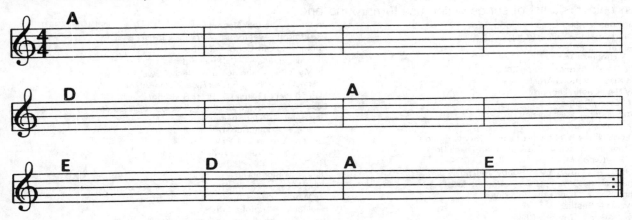

Written below is a list of songs which use 12 Bar Blues.

Be-bop-a-lula — Gene Vincent/John Lennon
Hound Dog — Elvis Presley
Johnny B. Goode — Chuck Berry
Boppin' the Blues — Blackfeather
The Wanderer — Dion
Going up the Country — Canned Heat
Makin your mind up — Bucks Fizz
Green Door — Shakin' Stevens
In the Summertime — Mungo Jerry
Rock Around the Clock — Bill Haley & The Comets
Barbara Ann — Beach Boys
Let's Stick Together — Brian Ferry
Long Tall Glasses (I Know I can Dance) — Leo Sayer
Blue Suede Shoes — Elvis Presley
School Days (Ring Ring Goes the Bell) — Chuck Berry
Roll Over Beethoven — Chuck Berry
Spirit in the Sky — Norman Greenbaum
Turn up your Radio — Masters Apprentices
Tutti Fruitt — Little Richard
Dizzy Miss Lizzy — Larry Williams/Beatles
I Can Help — Billy Swan
Rockin' Robin — Michael Jackson
The Walls Come Down — The Call

Get Down and Get With It — Slade
Good Golly Miss Molly — Little Richard
Lucille — Little Richard
In the Mood — Glenn Miller
Surfin' Safari — Beach Boys
Peppermint Twist — Sweet
Boogie Woogie Bugle Boy — Andrew Sisters/Bette Midler
I hear you Knocking — Dave Edmunds
Boy from New York City — Darts/Manhattan Transfer
Mountain of Love — Johnny Rivers
I Love to Boogie — T-Rex
Shake, Rattle & Roll — Bill Haley
Lady Rose — Mungo Jerry
Theme to Batman
Theme to Spiderman
Stuck in the Middle with you — Stealers Wheel
Hot Love — T-Rex
The Huckle Buck — Brendan Bower
Way Down — Elvis Presley
Peggy Sue — Buddy Holly
Jailhouse Rock — Elvis Presley
Green Door — Shakin' Stevens

SHEET MUSIC

Sheet music is generally arranged for piano and this can present problems for the bass guitarist. Piano music uses three staves, as such:

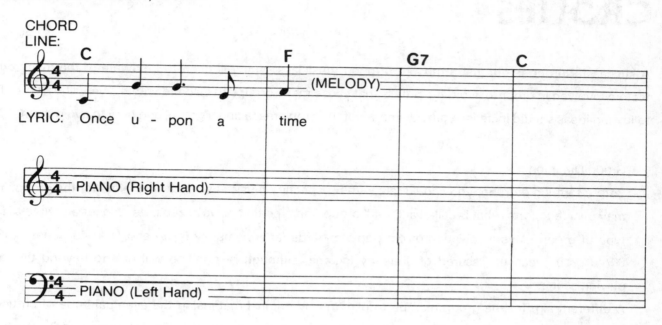

A bass player need only use the bass clef and/or the chord symbols to construct a bass line. Using the bass clef simply involves reading the notes as written, and in most cases this will provide a suitable bass line. Sometimes, however, it is not possible to read the given piano bass; e.g. when it includes chords (i.e. three or more notes played together) or notes beyond the range of the bass guitar.

In a situation involving chords, choose one chord note which blends in best with the bass line as a whole. For a note which is out of the bass guitar's range, either play its octave or choose another chord note to blend with the bass line.

If you choose to construct a bass line from the given chords of a piece of sheet music (i.e. not reading the bass clef) you can apply any of the approaches studied in Section $\overline{\text{III}}$.

CARS (Courtesy WEA)

APPENDIX FOUR –
GROUPS

A successful group is not just a mixture of good musicians. You will need to be aware of the many other factors involved in order to avoid the pitfalls that cause many groups to disband within a very short time. The following ideas should increase your awareness of the problems facing a group, and how to avoid them.

1. Group Direction

   Before forming a group, you should talk with prospective musicians about their aims for the group. You may decide to form what is called a '60/40' group; the type that plays at cabarets, dances and hotels. This type of group plays a selection of old pop standards (approximately 60%) and 'Top 40' tunes (40%). 60/40 groups can be assured of a steady income, although recognition will not go beyond the local playing scene.

   A different aim for the group may be to play mainly original material in the eventual hope of cutting a record and going on tours. Groups of this type generally do not make much money until they have become well known.

   If you are forming a new group you may find it more beneficial to play a 60/40 style to gain experience and money to invest in top quality equipment.

   Decide on the number of musicians, the type of instruments and the basic style of music before forming the group.

2. Music Choice

   The style of music you play must be one that is enjoyed by all group members (not just a majority vote). Listen to other bands playing their various different styles and take particular note of the audience reaction in order to gauge the appeal of each style. Once you have decided on a style, aim specifically towards the section of people who enjoy that type of music. This will immediately decrease the number of possible venues for you to play at; but remember that you cannot please everyone and you should therefore aim to play to the type of people whom you will please.

3. The Group Structure

   A group can be divided into 2 basic sections; a 'rhythm section' and a 'lead section'. The instruments of the rhythm section include drums, and bass (which lay down the basic beat), and rhythm guitar (which 'fills-out' the basic beat). These instruments must co-ordinate to provide the background rhythm; the 'tightness' of the group will depend on it.

   The lead section usually consists of lead guitar, vocals and keyboards (which may be used as either a lead or rhythm instrument). The lead instrument acts as a separate voice from the vocals and 'leads' in and out of each section or verse of a song (i.e. an introduction or a 'lead break').

   All instruments must work as a team, in order to provide a combined group sound.

4. Rehearsals

In a serious group you will spend more time rehearsing than doing anything else, so it is important to be properly organised. As far as possible, each session should have an objective which you should strive to achieve.

Remember that the performance of a song involves not only the music, but also sound balance and stage presentation. These facets should be practised as part of the rehearsal.

As well as group rehearsal, you should practice individually. Concentrate particularly on the harder sections of your songs, so that it will be easier to play them when working with the group. It is far more beneficial and time saving for each member to attend group practice with full knowledge of his part.

The underlying theme of all the above topics is one of group unity, both on and off the stage. This is essential if the group is to survive together as an effective musical unit.

COPYING BASS LINES FROM RECORDS

As a bass guitarist, you will sometimes be required to play a given bass line from a record (as compared to creating your own). Copying from records can be very difficult at first, so here are a few suggestions:

1. Your bass guitar should always be tuned to concert pitch (i.e. tune to a tuning fork or pitch pipes). This is necessary because most recorded music is at concert pitch.
2. Start with a simple bass line. Tape it onto a cassette so that you can play it many times over without damaging the record.
3. Listen carefully to the rhythm of the notes and determine the time signature of the piece. Once this is done, you can break the bass line into smaller phrases, or even down to one bar at a time.
4. Sing through the phrase and then try to locate those notes on the bass.
5. As you work through the bass line, try to determine the key of the music. This should help you to anticipate the notes as they come and perhaps locate a pattern into which they fall. For example, if you are working on a bass line which contains C#'s and F#'s, this will suggest the key of D major (see "Key Signatures" on page 95).
6. Quite often it is hard to distinguish the bass line (particularly in pre 80's recordings). One method to help highlight the bass line is to use a two speed recorder, i.e. record the song at the slower speed and play back at the faster speed. The bass line will sound clearer, but it will be an octave higher and twice as fast, so you will have to compensate accordingly.
7. Practice record copying (often referred to as 'transcribing') regularly, but not for a long period of time in each session as your concentration and hearing ability declines.

GLOSSARY OF MUSICAL TERMS

Accent — a sign, >, used to indicate a predominant beat.

Accidental — a sign used to show a temporary change in pitch of a note (i.e. sharp ♯ , flat ♭ , double sharp ✕ , double flat ♭♭ , or natural ♮). The sharps or flats in a key signature are not regarded as accidentals.

Additional notes — a note which is used in a riff, but does not belong to the scale upon which the riff is based (also see "passing notes").

Ad lib — to be played at the performer's own discretion.

Allegro — fast and lively.

Anacrusis — a note or notes occurring before the first bar of music (also called 'lead-in' or 'pick-up' notes).

Andante -- an easy walking pace.

Arpeggio — the playing of a chord in single note fashion.

Bar — a division of music occurring between two bar lines (also called a 'measure').

Bar line — a vertical line drawn across the staff which divides the music into equal sections called bars.

Bass — the lower regions of pitch

Bass clef — a sign placed at the beginning of the staff to fix the pitch of the notes placed on it. The bass clef is placed so that the fourth line indicates an F note.

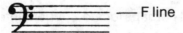 — F line

Bend — a technique which involves pushing a string upwards (or downwards), which raises the pitch of the fretted note being played.

'Blues' Scale — consisting of the I̅, ♭III̅, IV̅, V̅ and ♭VII̅ notes relative to the major scale.

Chord — a combination of three or more different notes played together.

Chord progression — a series of chords played as a musical unit (e.g. as in a song).

Chromatic scale — a scale ascending and descending in semitones.
e.g. C chromatic scale:

ascending: C   C♯   D   D♯   E   F   F♯   G   G♯   A   A♯   B   C

descending: C   B   B♭   A   A♭   G   G♭   F   E   E♭   D   D♭   C

Clef — a sign placed at the beginning of each staff of music which fixes the location of a particular note on the staff, and hence the location of all other notes. e.g.

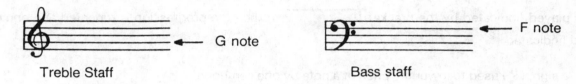

Treble Staff   ← G note   ← F note   Bass staff

Cliches — small musical phrases that are frequently used.

Coda — an ending section of music, signified by the sign ⊕ .

Common time — an indication of $\frac{4}{4}$ time — four quarter note beats per bar.

Compound time — occurs when the beat falls on a dotted note, which is thus divisible by three; e.g. $\frac{6}{8}$ $\frac{9}{8}$ $\frac{12}{8}$

D.C. al fine — a repeat from the beginning to the word 'fine'.

Dot — a sign placed after a note indicating that its time value is extended by a half. e.g.

♩ = 2 counts   ♩. = 3 counts

Double bar line — two vertical lines close together, indicating the end of a piece, or section thereof.

Double flat — a sign (♭♭) which lowers the pitch of a note by one tone.

Double sharp — a sign (✗) which raises the pitch of a note by one tone.

D.S. al fine — a repeat from the sign (indicated thus 𝄋) to the word 'fine'.

Duration — the time value of each note or strum (see 'Rhythm').

Dynamics — the varying degrees of softness (indicated by the term 'piano') and loudness (indicated by the term 'forte') in music.

Eighth note — a note with the value of half a beat in $\frac{4}{4}$ time, indicated thus ♪ (also called a quaver).

The eighth note rest, indicating half a beat of silence, is written: 𝄾

Enharmonic — describes the difference in notation, but not in pitch, of two notes; e.g.

F♯ and G♭ :- 

Fermata — a sign, ⌢ , used to indicate that a note or chord is held to the player's own discretion (also called 'pause sign').

First and second endings — signs used where two different endings occur. On the first time through ending one is played (indicated by the bracket $\overline{|^1\qquad}$); then the progression is repeated and ending two is played (indicated $\overline{|^2\qquad}$).

Flat — a sign, (♭) used to lower the pitch of a note by one semitone.

Form — the plan or layout of a song, in relation to the sections it contains; e.g. Binery form, containing an 'A section and a 'B' section (A B)
Ternary form, containing an 'A' section and a 'B' section, and then a repeat of the 'A' section (A B A).
The verse/chorus relationship in songs is an example of form.

Forte — loud. Indicated by the sign f

Free stroke — where the finger, after picking the string, does not come to rest on any other string

Half note — a note with the value of two beats in $\frac{4}{4}$ time, indicted thus: ♩ (also called a minum).

The half note rest, indicating two beats of silence, is written: ━■━ ⟵ third staff line.

Hammer-on — sounding a note by using only the left hand fingers (also called a 'slur').

Harmonics — a chime like sound created by lightly touching a vibrating string at certain points along the fret board.

Harmony — the simultaneous sounding of two or more different notes.

"I" — index finger. As used for identifying the right hand fingers.

Improvise — to perform spontaneously; i.e. not from memory or from a written copy.

Interval — the distance between any two notes of different pitches.

Key — describes the notes used in a composition in regards to the major or minor scale from which they are taken; e.g. a piece 'in the key of C major' describes the melody, chords, etc., as predominantly consisting of the notes C, D, E, F, G, A, and B — i.e. from the C scale.

Key signature — a sign, placed at the beginning of each stave of music, directly after the clef, to indicate the key of a piece. The sign consists of a certain number of sharps or flats, which represent the sharps or flats found in the scale of the piece's key: e.g.

 indicates a scale with F♯ and C♯ , which is D major; D E F♯ G A B C♯ D.
Therefore the key is D major.

Lead — the playing of single notes, as in a lead solo or melody line.

Ledger lines — small horizontal lines upon which notes are written when their pitch is either above or below the range of the staff, e.g.

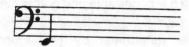

Legato — smoothly, well connected.

Lyric — words that accompany a melody.

"**m**" — middle finger. As used for identifying the right hand fingers.

Major scale — a series of eight notes in alphabetical order based on the interval sequence tone - **tone** - semitone - tone - tone - tone - semitone.

Melody — a succession of notes of varying pitch and duration, and having a recognizable musical shape.

Metronome — a device which indicates the number of beats per minute, and which can be adjusted in accordance to the desired tempo.
e.g. MM (Maelzel Metronome) ♩ = 60 — indicates 60 quarter note beats per minute.

Mode — a displaced scale e.g. playing through the C to C scale, but starting and finishing on the D note.

Moderato — at a moderate pace.

Modulation — the changing of key within a song (or chord progression).

Natural — a sign (♮) used to cancel out the effect of a sharp or flat. The word is also used to desribe the notes A, B, C, D, E, F and G; e.g. 'the natural notes'.

Notation — the written representation of music, by means of symbols (music on a staff), letters (as in chord and note names) and diagrams (as in chord illustrations).

Note — a single sound with a given pitch and duration.

Octave — the distance between any given note with a set frequency, and another note with exactly double that frequency. Both notes will have the same letter name;

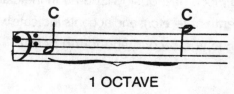

1 OCTAVE

Passing note — an additional note which connects two adjacent scale notes.

Phrase — a small group of notes forming a recognizable unit within a melody.

Pitch — the sound produced by a note, determined by the frequency of the string vibrations. The pitch relates to a note being referred to as 'high' or 'low'.

Plectrum (or Pick) — a small object (often of a triangular shape) made of plastic which is used to pick the strings of a bass guitar.

Position — a term used to describe the location of the left hand on the fret board. The left hand position is determined by the fret location of the first finger, e.g.
The 1st position refers to the 1st to 4th frets. The 3rd position refers to the 3rd to 6th frets and so on.

Quarter note - a note with the value of one beat in ⁴₄ time, indicated thus ♩ (also called a crotchet).

The quarter note rest, indicating one beat of silence, is written: 𝄽

Reggae — a Jamaican rhythm featuring an accent on the second and fourth beats (in ⁴₄ time).

Relative — a term used to describe the relationship between a major and minor key which share the same key signature; e.g. G major and E minor are relative keys both sharing the F♯ key signature.

Repeat signs — in music, used to indicate a repeat of a section of music, by means of two dots placed before a double bar line:

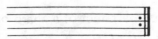

In chord progressions, a repeat sign ╱⁄, indicates an exact repeat of the previous bar.

Rest — the notation of an absence of sound in music.

Rest stroke — where the finger, after picking the string, comes to rest on the next string

Rhythm — the aspect of music concerned with tempo, duration and accents of notes (or chord strums). Tempo indicates the speed of a piece (fast or slow); duration indicates the time value of each note or strum (quarter note, eighth note, sixteenth note, etc.); and accents indicate which beat is more predominant (in rock, the first and third beats; in reggae, the second and fourth beats).

Riff — a pattern of notes that is repeated throughout a progression (song).

Root note — the note after which a chord or scale is named.

Scale Tone Chords — chords which are constructed from notes within a given scale.

Semitone — the smallest interval used in conventional music. On the bass guitar it is a distance of one fret.

Sharp — a sign (♯) used to raise the pitch of a note by one semitone.

Simple time — occurs when the beat falls on an undotted note, which is thus divisible by two.

Sixteenth note — a note with the value of quarter of a beat in ¾ time, indicated thus ♪ (also called a semiquaver).

The sixteenth note rest, indicating quarter of a beat of silence, is written: ⁊

Slide — a technique which involves a finger moving along the string to its new note. The finger maintains pressure on the string, so that a continuous sound is produced.

Slur — sounding a note by using only the left hand fingers. (an ascending slur is also called 'hammer-on'; a descending slur is also called 'flick-off').

Staccato — to play short and detached. Indicated by a dot placed above the note:

Staff — five parallel lines together with four spaces, upon which music is written.

Syncopation — the placing of an accent on a normally unaccented beat. e.g.:

```
      >   >                    >    >
1   2  3  4          1  + 2  +  3  +
```

Tablature — a system of writing music which represents the position of the player's fingers (not the pitch of the notes, but their position on the bass guitar). Notes are written using tablature thus:

Music notation   tablature   each line represents a string, and each number represents a fret.

Tempo — the speed of a piece.

Tie — a curved line joining two or more notes of the same pitch, where the second note(s) is not played, but its time value is added to that of the first note.

1/   2/

In example two, the first note is held for seven counts.

Timbre — a quality which distinguishes a note produced on one instrument from the same note produced on any other instrument (also called 'tone colour'). A given note on the bass guitar will sound different (and therefore distinguishable) from the same pitched note on piano, violin, flute, etc. There is usually also a difference in timbre from one bass guitar to another.

Time signature — a sign at the beginning of a piece which indicates, by means of figures, the number of beats per bar (top figure), and the type of note receiving one beat (bottom figure).

Tone — a distance of two frets; i.e. the equivalent of two semitones.

Transposition — the process of changing music from one key to another.

Treble — the upper regions of pitch in general.

Treble clef — a sign placed at the beginning of the staff to fix the pitch of the notes placed on it. The treble clef (also called 'G clef') is placed so that the second line indicates a G note:

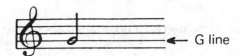

←— G line

Tremelo (pick tremelo) — a technique involving rapid pick movement on a given note.

Triplet — a group of three notes played in the same time as two notes of the same kind.

Eighth note triplet

Vibrato — a technique which involves pushing a string up and down, like a rapid series of short bends.

Wedge mark — indicates pick direction; e.g.:   V = down pick   Λ = up pick

Whole note — a note with the value of four beats in $\frac{4}{4}$ time, indicated thus ○ (also called a semibreve).

The whole note rest, indicating four beats of silence, is written: ——■ ←— 4th staff line.